CW01191723

Copyright © whatculture.com 2016. All Rights Reserved.

Published by What Culture.

All rights reserved. This book may not be reproduced, in whole or in any part, in any form, without written permission from the publisher or author.

This book is set in Garamond, and Calibri.

10 9 8 7 6 5 4 3 2 1

This book was printed and bound in the United Kingdom.

ISBN 978-1-326-60119-5

SHOCKING WRESTLING PLANS YOU WON'T BELIEVE ALMOST HAPPENED

COMPILED BY:

James Dixon

WRITTEN BY:

Ben Cooke

James Dixon

Simon Gallagher

Grahame Herbert

Lewis Howse

Jamie Kennedy

Kenny McIntosh

Ross Tweddell

WITH:

Jim Cornette

Dan Madigan

Vince Russo

George J Rutherford

ARTWORK BY:

Bob Dahlstrom

Benjamin Richardson

CONTENTS

- 9   **FOREWORD** by Jim Cornette

MATCHES

- 15   Roddy Piper vs. OJ Simpson
  Mankind vs. The Undertaker
  Shaquille O'Neal vs. The Big Show
  Ric Flair vs. Hulk Hogan
- 16   Mike Tyson vs. Triple H
- 17   Chris Jericho vs. Mickey Rourke
  Shawn Michaels vs. Vince McMahon
  Hulk Hogan vs. Shawn Michaels
- 18   Eric Bischoff vs. Vince McMahon
- 19   Shawn Michaels vs. The British Bulldog
  Exploding Cage: X-Pac vs. Kane
  The Sheild vs. The Brothers of Destruction
- 20   The Undertaker vs. Abyss
- 21   Andre the Giant vs. Mr. Perfect
  The Ultimate Warrior vs. Bill Goldberg
- 22   The Rock vs. Bill Goldberg
  WWE vs. Jackass
- 23   Sting vs. Steve Austin
- 24   Hulk Hogan vs. Giant Gonzalez
- 25   Rick Steiner vs. Ric Flair
- 27   Bret Hart vs. Hulk Hogan
- 28   Mordecai vs. The Undertaker
- 29   Justin Bieber, The Big Show & John Cena vs. The Wyatts
  Paul Heyman vs. Paul Bearer
- 30   Dana White vs. Vince McMahon
- 31   Bret Hart vs. Shawn Michaels

FEATURE by George J. Rutherford
- 34   10 Things You Learn As A WWE Creative Writer

REBRANDING

- 40   Chilly McFreeze
- 42   'The Game' Owen Hart
- 43   The Millionaire's Club Avengers
  George W. Bush
  Mason The Mutilator
- 44   Space Corps Holly
- 45   Mark Jindrak in Evolution
  Hirohito
  'Professor X' Hade Vansen
- 46   Naked Goldust
- 47   Deaf C.M. Punk
  The Posse Unchained
- 48   Triple H in the nWo
  Christian's Blue Dot
- 49   'Cowboy' Bret Hart
  Tori - Sable's Sister
  'G.I. Joe' Scott Hall
- 50   The Gobbledy-Taker
- 52   The Shielded Shield
- 53   Psychopath Samoa Joe
  Heel John Cena
  Louie 'Chris Farley' Spicolli
  Deaf, Mute Edge
- 54   Comedy Rusev
  Ric Flair is Spartacus
  'Silverback' Mark Henry
  The Hunchbacks
- 55   Mighty Mouse
  Muhammad Hassan - World Champion
  Maria Montana
- 56   The Ultimate Vader
- 58   Baron Von Bava
- 59   Albert Steele

FEATURE by Vince Russo
- 62   10 Insights Into Working With Vince McMahon

BOOKING

- 68   Vader - WWF Champion
  John Cena Cleans Up The Streets
  Intergalactic Warfare
  The Tubby Vampire
- 69   Sylvain Grenier - Main Event Superstar
  The Return of the Four Horsemen
- 70   Tyson and Hogan! Tyson and Hogan!
  The Ballad of Triple H and Stephanie
- 71   "I Still Remember"
  JTG and "Self"
- 72   Sting Was Nearly "The Third Man"
- 73   WrestleMania III's "Plan B"
- 74   Chyna - WWF Champion
  Who Killed Mr. McMahon?
- 75   John Cena Killed The Nexus
  Jericho Wanted To Tattoo Punk

76	SummerSlam '92 Rebooked
77	The Tragedy of Magnum TA
78	The Goldberg Blueprint
	The Mystery of GTV
79	The Real Kane
	The Game Changer
80	Kizarny and Vince The Clown
81	El Matador - WWF Champion
	Mr. G and the G-Spots
	Sable and the Hummer
82	Tank Abbott - WCW Champion
	Kevin Dun's Influence
	Hale Baby
83	Brian Pillman Was Going To Steal Goldust's Wife
	Christian Was Behind For Jeff Hardy's Accidents
	Raven's Seven Deadly Sins
	Vince Russo's TNA Invasions
84	Mark Henry Was Going To Break The Streak
85	The Ultimate Warrior's Heel Turn
86	Judy Bagwell - Multi-Time Champion
87	The Long-Term Plan For The nWo
88	The Original Plan For WrestleMania XXX
	Rusev and Summer's Wedding
89	Mankind's Mommy
90	Vince Russo's Worked Shoots
91	John Cena's Rap Battles

FEATURE by Dan Madigan
94   A Few Thoughts On The Business...

RISQUE

100	Brock Lesnar Was Pitched As A Homosexual
101	Ric Flair - Dirty Grandpa
	Incestuous Ken Shamrock
	The Blonde Bitch Project
102	The Burchills
	Sable 4 Undertaker
	Melina The Man
103	The Original WWE Gay Wedding
105	Batista - Child of Rape
	Owen 4 Debra
	Vince 4 Stephanie
	Goldust's Breasts

FEATURE by George J. Rutherford
108   The Wisdom of Dusty Rhodes

DEFECTORS

112	The British Bulldog
113	Shawn Michaels
	The Ultimate Warrior
	Genichiro Tenryu
114	Macho Man and Hulk Hogan
115	NFL Stars

FEATURE by Scott Carlson
118   10 Wrestlers Who Nearly Defected During The Monday Night War

BACKSTAGE

124	Bret Hart Was Nearly Part Of The Kliq
	WCW's Millennium Show Plans
125	Randy Savage Tried To Buy WCW
126	John Cena Was Nearly Fired
	WWE British Office
	Divas SmackDown
127	Eugene Almost Had A Movie
128	Throttling Vince McMahon Is Bad For Your Push
129	Ludicrous Reality Show Pitches
	WCW Raw
	ECW Online

FOREWORD

BY JIM CORNETTE...

When I was first contacted to write the foreword for the book you are about to read, I was somewhat puzzled by the concept. An entire book of bad pro wrestling ideas? There would surely be no shortage of material, but I was uncertain as to whether anyone would want to read it. However, after seeing a rough draft of the manuscript, I can actually say that reading this colossal compendium of idiotic ideas, preposterous plans and brainstorms of bullshit might be more entertaining than watching most of today's actual wrestling shows.

Your editors have compiled a fascinating tome of the worst inspirations ever to come to the mind of man--from the lowest of the unknown faces on wrestling's totem pole of "creative" writers to the diarrhoea of the keyboard spewed forth by the man himself, the undisputed champion of booking blunders and career-killing concepts, the Archbishop of Talent Bury, Vince Russo. Are all of these stories true? I can't testify to that in court, but I know enough of them are to lend plenty of credibility to the ones I HADN'T heard before. Yes, from bad judgement to brain damage, it's all here.

To be perfectly fair, sometimes in wrestling you HAVE to try to make chicken salad out of chicken shit. Over a 25 year period, I personally wrote and produced 200 hours of Smoky Mountain Wrestling TV and over 600 live events, 300 hours of Ohio Valley Wrestling TV and almost 1000 live events, plus contributed to hundreds of hours of WWE, WCW, and Ring of Honour TV shows, live events and pay-per-views. I never pitched or produced an idea I thought was bad--at the time--although a number of them sure turned out that way in execution. Sometimes, things just get lost in the translation.

But as you will see from reading this book, as the years pass, things get worse--much worse--and a younger wrestling fan may not understand why. Here's the scoop, and unfortunately, this is not a situation that is likely to be rectified.

In the 1980's, bad ideas came from usually successful people blinded by ego or a personal dislike of a talent they were trying to screw over, or those that were backed in a corner by circumstances or just plain burned out. Pro wrestling was controlled, as it had been since the dawn of time, by wrestling people with years, even decades of on-the-job training and experience, who had drawn money and become famous as promoters or performers themselves. These men's paychecks and livelihoods depended on the continued success and popularity of all wrestling in general and their own promotions in particular, so they were not only careful to examine ideas closely before they were executed, but to police their talent rosters to make sure that no one did anything to damage the credibility or believability of the sport. But, as you will soon read, even when these folks had bad ideas, they at least--somewhat--made sense upon closer examination of the conditions and personalities at the time.

But as the 1980's drew to a close, wrestling had gotten TOO successful for its own good, and outsiders--businessmen, corporate America--discovered there was a lot of money to be made in the game. Turner Broadcasting purchased Jim Crockett Promotions to form World Championship Wrestling in 1988, and in doing so, with access to literally every smart, successful and talented booker and promoter of the previous few decades, hired as the captain of their soon-to-be sinking ship a former Pizza Hut executive named Jim Herd. Herd's credentials in wrestling were that 20 years before, he had been the director of a TV wrestling show in St. Louis. More importantly, his wife was best friends with the wife of a high-ranking TBS executive. And the bad-idea floodgates were opened.

The Hunchbacks, the Ding Dongs, Robocop--Herd's "creative" ideas were legendary, and he set WCW on the path to an unprecedented seven-year money losing streak, giving Vince McMahon and the then-WWF the same amount of time and a clear field to emerge as the undisputed leader of the pro wrestling world.

Now, Vince and his merry band had some rotten ideas themselves--Gobbledy Gook--and since Vince always wanted to be Walt Disney instead of promoting wrestling, most of these ideas centred around bad comedy and making wrestling look phony. However, when the chairman of the evil empire actually DID get some competition, these earlier concepts looked like Shakespeare.

Eric Bischoff was chosen to guide WCW in 1994, and quite by accident, he was able to do what no other WCW head had done--convince Turner Broadcasting to actually spend money on the wrestling company. He hired a lot of former stars of McMahon's away, and began winning the ratings battle. McMahon, losing a fight for the first time in his life, panicked and gave the keys to the car to the aforementioned Russo, and we were headed for disaster.

The battle for supremacy saw both companies disregard their entire futures for a rating that week. Russo's trashy, business-exposing, ADD-ridden "booking" hotshotted the WWF and forced Bischoff and his men to go as far or farther in response. The "Monday Night Wars" led to the biggest financial business pro wrestling had ever done in America-- for about two years. Then, as all the wrestling veterans knew would happen, the constant hotshotting and barrage of angles and screwjobs led to finishes and angles being overdone and devalued, burned up hundreds of talents and decades' worth of content, numbed the fans to injuries and violent spectacles, and created a situation where there was nothing left to follow it all with. When the companies lost control and things headed south--for WCW, it was 2000, when they lost $60 million, for WWF it was 2001 when they turned Steve Austin heel and botched the WCW "invasion" angle after buying the business for fire-sale prices--it was too late to go back. Fifteen years later, the industry still hasn't recovered from the damage done by the Monday Night Wars, and likely never shall.

Because one more coffin nail was to come. While still riding high, the now-WWE went public, selling stock in the company. Vince's daughter Stephanie McMahon, fresh out of college and about to be sold the ultimate bill of goods by accomplished power-grabber HHH, was appointed the "head of WWE creative", and began hiring not ex-wrestlers or bookers to work under her, but instead "writers" with college degrees and experience working in "real" television. This is comparable to me being hired as a pilot for Delta Airlines because I flew coach once.

The comedy writers, bolstered by the fact that the corporate owners of all these big promotions had actually been admitting wrestling was a work for years, had no knowledge of how wrestling worked or respect for its credibility, and began pitching one idea after another meant to elicit a chuckle or a gasp without any thought as to whether anyone would either believe it, or pay to see it. You will see in this book the results of these jock-sniffing pretenders' musings. Pro wrestling degenerated into a bad acid trip where even the stuff that actually made TV was often untenable for anyone with a love or respect of the profession to watch.

It's been that way since, and because you can't put the toothpaste back in the tube or un-ring the bell, it's likely never to change. Pro wrestling will always be around in some form, but there's no way it can ever reach the mainstream popularity it enjoyed either on TV or as a live attraction most of the time from the dawn of the 20th century to about 1988-- you can't get people to emotionally invest in what they now know is a completely pre-planned exhibition instead of a physical conflict. The UFC has become the most successful pro wrestling promotion in the world--the wrestling companies are pretty much producers of weekly free TV content now.

So having said that, read this book quickly, because the way things are going, if you peruse these stories five years from now, you may be sitting there in 2021 saying to yourself, "Rotten ideas? Hell, this stuff is great compared to what I saw on TV last week." And you'll probably be right

Jim Cornette
Louisville, KY
March 2016

MATCHES

THE BOUTS THAT NEVER WERE...

14

RODDY PIPER VS. OJ SIMPSON

Despite the failed experiment of football player Lawrence Taylor wrestling in the main event of WrestleMania XI, the WWF were not put off by the idea of putting celebrities in the ring to square off with their wrestlers again. In early 1996, Bruce Prichard (him again) pitched one of the most out-there ideas in company history: OJ Simpson versus Roddy Piper at WrestleMania XII.

While Simpson – like Taylor – originally made his name playing football, he was far more renowned for being accused of murdering his ex-wife Nicole Brown Simpson and waiter Ronald Lyle Goldman. For a while in 1995 the court case was the most talked-about thing in the entire world, and it would not be a stretch to say that for one year, Simpson was the most (in)famous man on the planet. Prichard wanted to capitalise on Simpson's notoriety by putting him in the ring with company icon Piper, which he figured would make WrestleMania XII the most watched pay-per-view event of all time.

Evidently Vince McMahon agreed and authorised his team to enter negotiations with Simpson's representatives. They talked, briefly, but no agreement materialised, leaving Piper without an opponent. As luck would have it, Scott Hall flunked a drug test and was out of WrestleMania, so the WWF inserted Piper in his place for a bout with resident androgyne Goldust.

Piper beat the snot out of him at 'Mania in a Hollywood Backlot Brawl, during which the WWF cut to footage of the OJ Simpson car chase and claimed Piper and Goldust were behind the wheel of the vehicles. No doubt, they would have done something similar had the real OJ wrestled on the show, because in the world of the WWF, nothing is off limits.

MANKIND VS. UNDERTAKER ON ALCATRAZ ISLAND

Gimmick matches aren't exactly a new thing in wrestling: who can forget the undignified sight of the Big Show squeezed into a sumo mawashi? But Jim Ross almost organised the most ingenious gimmick setting of all time when he pitched the idea of having Mankind and the Undertaker fight on Alcatraz Island prior to their first Boiler Room Brawl. Sadly, something as boring as bureaucracy got in the way: "We couldn't get it cleared legally at that time to do it. It was a rough idea with no final, final details and in hindsight might not have been one of my better suggestions. However, it did sound good at the time and packed plenty of 'sizzle'."

SHAQUILLE O'NEAL VS. THE BIG SHOW

A month after being traded from the Phoenix Suns to the Cleveland Cavaliers, iconic baller and terrible actor Shaq O'Neal hosted Raw, ending with a toe-to-toe square-up to the Big Show. After attempting to trade chokeslams, Shaq shouldered Show out of the ring, kicking off rumours that they would settle their beef in the ring. It was slow going, but two and a half years later the story broke that the pair would collide when Shaq announced he was in discussions to join the bill at WrestleMania XXVIII. Despite Shaq confirming it on three other separate occasions, WWE denied the deal in a statement, leaving one of the most compelling what ifs for monster fans.

RIC FLAIR VS. HULK HOGAN

When the WWF signed NWA kingpin Ric Flair in 1991, fans immediately salivated at the prospect of a showdown between he and WWF icon Hulk Hogan. It was the most logical pairing in the world and a dream match that fans worldwide had wanted to see for years. Vince McMahon decided to do a few test runs of the match with the intention being to put it on the WrestleMania VIII card as the main event. Unfortunately, McMahon was not impressed with what he saw. "We left it too late," he grumbled, disappointed with the relatively tepid audience response and poor turnout. The match was shelved and 'Mania plans were altered as a result.

MIKE TYSON VS. TRIPLE H

By 2001, having a boxing match in the ring wasn't exactly a ground-breaking idea (it had been done in the WWWF in the 70s with Gorilla Monsoon), but having a wrestling box someone as potentially dangerous to their health as Mike Tyson certainly was. Yet, that was one of the ideas thrown around when the WWF were looking for someone from outside of the business to take on Triple H at WrestleMania X-Seven. It made sense both fiscally and from a storyline perspective. Tyson had done big business with the WWF in 1998 helping the company build Steve Austin as a global megastar, and Triple H was one of his former partners in DX—who Tyson had turned on—who wanted revenge.

The pitch came at the height of Tyson's post-peak controversy (one of them, anyway), when he was fighting no-hopers, testing positive for marijuana and refusing to stop punching an opponent after the referee had stopped the fight. He was a loose cannon, in other words, but that didn't faze Triple H - who had also been pitched fights with Ray Lewis and a Japanese MMA fighter.

As he explains: "We were going to do six rounds. I don't remember if it was going to be full boxing rules, or whether I was wearing gloves. But it ended up being a deal where the whole thing just would have been a ludicrous amount of money, and it got pushed off. I wrestled 'Taker [instead] and that ended up becoming one of my favourite matches."

Ultimately nothing came of it because Tyson could not get cleared to compete in a wrestling ring while he was actively boxing, but just imagine what a spectacle that could have been. It certainly would have ranked above Floyd Mayweather vs. Big Show.

CHRIS JERICHO VS. MICKEY ROURKE

Mickey Rourke's preparation for his Oscar-nominated performance in The Wrestler is fairly well-documented. He was famously put through eight months of conditioning and training by former Wild Samoan Afa Anoa'i, preparation which clearly gave him the confidence to actually consider a stint in the ring. His short feud on WWE television with Chris Jericho was initially intended to lead to them wrestling at *WrestleMania XXV*, before the actor killed the angle dead by letting the cat out of the bag too early. Rourke let plans slip during interviews, and his people panicked, worrying that association with the tacky and controversial WWE (this was only 18-months after Benoit) could cost him his Best Actor nomination. In the end, he didn't win anyway, but he and almost everyone else believed he had a great chance of doing so and he had no intention of jeopardising that. Instead, Jericho faced Hall of Famers Ricky Steamboat, Superfly Jimmy Snuka, and Roddy Piper (with plans to also have Jerry Lawler appear in order to tick off a 'Mania appearance from this bucket list nixed by Vince McMahon), with Rourke settling for role watching from ringside. Sadly/mercifully Randy the Ram has never considered an in-ring appearance since.

SHAWN MICHAELS VS. VINCE MCMAHON

Shawn Michaels returned to WWE in 2002 after over four years out with a back injury and battling substance abuse issues. The company had wanted to bring Michaels back on several occasions in the past (he did have a recurring role as WWF Commissioner for a time) but HBK's 'demons' always managed to get in the way. Vince called Michaels in May 2002 about coming in and doing a stint with the nWo, who were by on their last legs by that point. Michaels agreed and briefly partook, then Kevin Nash tore his quad and the group disbanded soon afterwards. Open to wrestling another match, Shawn suggested that he work a programme with Vince McMahon. Michaels had worked some gimmicky street fights for his indie promotion TWA and felt that he could do it with WWE, as long as it was with somebody like Vince where he could use copious shortcuts to hide is lack of ring conditioning. Plus, it meant there wouldn't be the expectation of a classic match, taking the pressure off. The storyline was going to be Shawn defending the honour of wrestlers that Vince pushed too hard and subsequently got injured (like he and Nash). Vince came back with the idea of Michaels having the street fight against Triple H instead. Although sceptical, Shawn eventually agreed and the rest is history.

HULK HOGAN VS. SHAWN MICHELS

At the 2005 edition of *SummerSlam* fans were treated to a first-time-ever match between two legendary company icons, Shawn Michaels and Hulk Hogan. The build to what WWE were rightly calling a "Dream Match" was memorable. It started with a Michaels superkick to Hogan following a bout where the two teamed together, then saw Michaels play heel for the first time since his 2002 comeback. He was wonderful in the role, slipping back into his old arrogant 'Heartbreak Kid' ways with ease. One memorable segment in Canada saw Michaels receive a volley of abuse from the locals who had not forgiven him for his part in the Montreal Screwjob eight years prior, with chants of "We Want Bret!" drowning out his promo. When Hart's music played the building erupted in one of the most memorable pops of all time, but it was soon revealed as a brilliant ruse from Michaels designed to get heat. Conspicuous by his absence during the hype was Hogan, who was proving his typically difficult self to work with behind the scenes. Initial plans were for a three match series between the two veterans that would see them exchanging wins before a rubber match at the following year's *WrestleMania*. But Hogan refused to put Michaels over and the decision was made to keep Hogan happy by letting him beat Michaels at *SummerSlam*, prematurely ending their series. Michaels took umbrage to Hogan's machinations and spent the entire bout overselling to the point of absurdity. Hogan was helpless to stop Michaels showing him up as he flailed and spun around the ring like an out of control yo-yo, and the pair never worked together again after that.

ERIC BISCHOFF VS. VINCE MCMAHON

It must be difficult for younger wrestling fans to grasp, but the the-World Wrestling Federation were not the number one promotion in the world in 1997 if you judged success on the weekly Monday night television ratings war. Rather it was Ted Turner's WCW, fronted by slick obnoxious Vice President Eric Bischoff, which was dominating the industry. Bischoff was so confident that WCW was soon going to put the WWF out of business that he frequently bragged about it to those around him, joking about hiring McMahon for a menial job with WCW.

But Bischoff reckoned without the red hot Steve Austin, not to mention the impact Mike Tyson would have on the WWF's programming. Tyson—who Bischoff had passed up on in 1997—was helping the WWF promote Austin to the mainstream, and it was working. When Vince McMahon became an onscreen character as well, the perfect heel foil to Austin' blue-collar babyface, the results were spectacular. On April 13, 1998, a show-long angle building to a McMahon-Austin match helped the WWF to finally turn the tide, with Raw beating Nitro for the first time in 84-weeks.

Bischoff played down the significance of the WWF's victory but his actions told another story. A few weeks later he went on *Nitro* and threw out a grandstand challenge, telling McMahon to come and fight him man-on-man at upcoming WCW pay-per-view *Slamboree*. It was a desperate attempt from Bischoff to convince viewers to part with their cash on the hollow promise of a showdown between the two most powerful men in wrestling. Surely it was never going to happen; McMahon was not about to help his competition by walking through the doors of WCW and giving them a major interest spike in their increasingly-stale by fighting Bischoff, was he?

According to many of McMahon's former employees, he was. So incensed was Vince by the upstart Bischoff's arrogance that he planned to call his bluff, even if it would have achieved nothing else other than promoting WCW as the place to be. If Vince had shown up, fans would equate WCW PPV events as a platform for unpredictability, only helping them in the future.

According to Vince Russo, who was McMahon's lead writer at the time: "Regardless of the fact that Eric and WCW would have greatly benefited from this publicity stunt, because it was a WCW pay-per-view, the business of it didn't even cross Vince's mind at the time. As a man, he was challenged, and his instinct was to answer the call. Vince was dead-set om showing up and fighting Eric. Trust me – the boss was serious. I could hear it in his words and I could see it in his eyes – he wasn't kidding. However, there was one small problem – the pay-per-view landed on the exact same day that Stephanie was graduating from Boston University. After some deliberation, Vince made the right decision and went to his beloved daughter's ceremony."

In the end, McMahon turned the tables and said he would fight Bischoff, but in a parking lot or a field somewhere rather than a WWF or WCW show. Bischoff never responded because his challenge was pure bravado. He knew McMahon would not come, it was nothing more than a cheap publicity stunt, the sort of thing that made WCW look foolish and second-rate. The scrap never ended up happening, but it's crazy to think that Vince McMahon seriously considered it. Give Eric Bischoff some credit for one thing, he certainly managed to get inside the head of his main rival.

SHAWN MICHAELS VS. BRITISH BULLDOG

Prior to the day of the event, the plan for the main event of UK-only pay-per-view *One Night Only* was for hometown hero The British Bulldog to retain his European Championship by defeating the despised Shawn Michaels, sending the sold-out Manchester crowd home happy.

Because McMahon had told Smith weeks earlier that he was winning the match, the Brit was confident the result was set in stone and told the local press he was dedicating the match to his sister Tracy, who was dying, ravaged by cancer aged just 26. Smith should have known better than to take a promoter's word as gospel, because just hours before the match McMahon found him and revealed he was changing the finish. Instead of Davey winning, Shawn would now be going over for the title.

"It was shock," said Smith's wife Diana, "I thought, 'You bastards! Why are they doing this to him in England? Where does that leave him?' There was something in the works then and we didn't know it."

McMahon explained to Smith how he wanted to build towards a rematch when the WWF toured England again in April the following year, and he felt Shawn winning the title would be a more emotive story than Smith simply retaining his gold. Smith had no choice to comply with McMahon's orders, but in an era before cell phones he was unable to pass the news on to his family. Tracy was so upset by the shock of her brother's defeat that she burst into a flood of tears, devastating the rest of the family. Smith was hurt the most by her reaction, unable to forgive himself for failing to live up to his promise.

Reaction amongst the wrestlers was typically knee-jerk. Adversaries of Michaels—and there were many—were convinced that he had politicked McMahon to change the finish in order to stick it to the Hart Foundation and show Bret Hart who was boss. That the result happened to change around the same time as Michaels had declared to a stunned locker room that he was no longer willing to do jobs for any of them, served as irrefutable evidence to some.

But the changed finish had little to do with Michaels, it was a McMahon judgment call. He was preparing to tell Bret Hart that he wanted to cut him loose or reduce his contract and suspected the discussion was not going to go well. McMahon decided to double down on Shawn Michaels in case the fall-out from the Hart contract discussions ultimately led to Smith leaving the WWF too. He was immobilising the Hart Foundation, weakening their presence as to ensure the likely loss of Hart would have as minimal impact on his company as possible. He was proven right about how things would go with Hart, a relationship with ended two months later with the infamous Montreal Screwjob. Davey Boy left with Hart, and by the April UK return *Mayhem in Manchester*, Michaels was on the shelf injured too, so the mooted rematch never happened.

EXPLODING CAGE: X-PAC VS. KANE

Keen to extend his feud with Kane in 2000, X-Pac pitched the idea of he and the 'Big Red Machine' facing off in an Exploding Barbed Wire Cage Match. Even deep into the Attitude Era, that would have been pretty out-there for the WWF. Incredibly, they considered the idea and actually tested out the explosives, before deciding that it wasn't going to work. Presumably they realised an arena full of people and high explosives weren't easy bedfellows. WWE has never contemplated a match of that nature since, rarely using barbed wire and never foraying into the realms of matches involving explosives.

SHIELD VS. BROTHERS OF DESTRUCTION

The night after *WrestleMania 29* The Undertaker was attacked by popular new renegade faction The Shield, in an angle designed to build to a future programme down the line. A few weeks later on *Smack-Down* in the UK, Undertaker made a surprise in-ring appearance opposite The Shield, again designed to lead to a PPV encounter. Unfortunately, the aging 'Dead Man' was injured taking The Shield's trademark triple-powerbomb bump through a ringside table, putting him on the shelf and nixing plans for Undertaker to reunite with his storyline brother Kane to battle the trio at *SummerSlam*.

THE UNDERTAKER VS. ABYSS

With Abyss's contract coming up for renewal in 2006, Tommy Dreamer served as a broker between the TNA star and WWE, which resulted in John Laurinaitis offering Abyss a deal. He was promised a big push, which included working a program with The Undertaker that would culminate in a match at WrestleMania 22.

You can see why the pair were identified as appropriate dance partners: both were billed as the most feared stars in their respective companies, both had unusual sibling storylines, and both were long-running foundation figures in the promotion they worked for.

Unfortunately for fans of creepy giant-on-giant action, Abyss got cold feet about leaving TNA and pulled out of the deal at the last minute.

Abyss claims not to regret it: "I absolutely 1,000 percent would make the same decision again. I absolutely have no regrets whatsoever. Being a part of TNA since the beginning is something that I am extremely proud of. I'm not saying other places aren't great places to go work, but for me the decision to stay on that occasion and several others is that I love TNA.

"I am TNA through and through and I always will be. I did have opportunities to go other places and I am proud that I was afforded that opportunity. The reason I stayed was for loyalty and no other reason. Not stage fright as Tommy joked in that interview, it had completely to do with the fact the I love TNA through and through.

"The company has treated me fantastic over the decade plus years I have been there. From Dixie to everyone there I am really happy there. I wanted to stay there and help build the company, be a part of something that I was with since the ground up. There is nowhere else in the World I could go and say that. That was the reason that I stayed and I have zero regrets. If I was asked to do it over again a 100 times I would do it 100 times."

ANDRE THE GIANT VS. MR. PERFECT

The final time fans caught a glimpse of Andre the Giant competing in WWF rings he departed as a conquered champion at WrestleMania VI following a WWF Tag Team Championship defeat alongside Haku to Demolition. Andre, a heel for the previous three years due to his association with the hated Bobby Heenan, delighted fans in Toronto's SkyDome by laying a beating on his manager. Andre departed as the loveable giant that fans had grown to know and love prior to his defection to the Heenan Family, never to compete on WWF television again.

But it was not his last ever match. Nor was it even supposed to be his final WWF outing. In 1991, there were plans for Andre to return to WWF rings once he had recovered from knee surgery. Onscreen the WWF's newest giant Earthquake was given storyline credit for injuring Andre's knee in an angle shot for Superstars on May 6th. The plan was to have Andre to come back and work a series with Earthquake, in addition to systematically dismantling his former Heenan Family stablemates, starting with Mr. Perfect.

Andre had involved himself in Perfect's business at WrestleMania VII, assisting the Big Boss Man in a post-match brawl that appeared to be building towards a future program. A few months later the match was set for a Wrestling Challenge taping on July 30, 1991 in Portland, Oregon, a full fifteen months since his last WWF outing.

Unfortunately, Andre was not recovered enough from his surgery to work a match, and his opponent Perfect was similarly crocked, suffering from a back injury brought about by his high-impact, big-bumping style. The WWF decided to save Andre's return for later in the year and instead had him assist Jim Neidhart in an untelevised victory over Iraqi-sympathising heel Sgt. Slaughter. Perfect was only able to manage a brief bump-free squash match victory over jobber Mark Thomas.

With Perfect taking over a year off following his SummerSlam defeat to Bret Hart the following month, the match with Andre never took place. Nor did Andre's return. After seconding comedy tandem the Bushwhackers for their SummerSlam '91 clash with Earthquake and his equally gargantuan partner Typhoon, Andre announced his retirement from the ring.

But Andre did not retire. Instead he went to All Japan Pro Wrestling and worked in a series of multi-man matches. Andre had suffered from acromegaly all his life and had already lived far beyond what most doctors predicted, but the condition was beginning to take its toll and limited Andre's movements significantly in those final bouts. However, such was the respect AJPW promoter Shohei Baba had for Andre that he still paid him $15,000 per week to essentially just walk to the ring and stand on the apron.

ULTIMATE WARRIOR VS. BILL GOLDBERG

The wheels were falling off the WCW wagon long before the company had the brainwave to turn Bill Goldberg heel. At *The Great American Bash* in June 2000, Goldberg—one of the only popular babyfaces the promotion had left—went rogue, and fans were sickened. The negative reaction was not down to a stellar heel turn, it was because fans didn't want to boo Goldberg. He was the one man WCW had protected in the booked who they could rally behind as the man to take the company out of the doldrums. Shortly after Goldberg's ill-advised turn, Vince Russo reached out to The Ultimate Warrior, a man last seen stinking up rings with Hulk Hogan in their infamously bad *Halloween Havoc '98* clash. Russo intended that Goldberg would become a proverbial wrecking ball, once again blazing a trail through the entire roster and looking unstoppable as he had done during his rewarding 1998 babyface run. Then with everyone beaten, Warrior would show up and promise to put an end to Goldberg's reign of tyranny. By mid-2000 WCW was so far gone that it is unlikely one match would have saved them, but it definitely would have been a marquee bout. There was only one problem. Fans refused to boo Goldberg. There was an overwhelming feeling that WCW had dropped the ball with him by ending his win streak against Kevin Nash at *Starrcade '98*, and due to this a lot of fans watching wanted to see him succeed in avenging that defeat and getting hot again like he had been in 1998 when he was on top of the world. By August he was babyface again, nixing all plans for the match.

THE ROCK VS. BILL GOLDBERG

In 2003, WWE had major plans for the long-awaited debut of former WCW phenomenon Bill Goldberg. Originally he was set to embark upon a long term feud with The Rock leading to a trio of matches, the last of which was scheduled to take place at *SummerSlam*. However, from the offset the entire series proved problematic. Their first match was going to take place at *WrestleMania XIX*, but Goldberg did not agree to terms with WWF until it was too late to build a program, and by then Rock had already signed on to work with the recently-returned Steve Austin. The match was postponed until *Backlash*, with Goldberg's debut coming the night after *WrestleMania* on *Raw*. The match at *Backlash* was an underwhelming affair that WWE fans quickly turned on. They booed Goldberg out of the building, feeling him to be a mercenary who only joined the company for the money, as opposed to The Rock who was one of their own. WWE did not want to run the bout again, and shortly after their first encounter The Rock departed WWE to continue his career in Hollywood, leaving the *SummerSlam* plans redundant. As such, WWE decided to focus its *SummerSlam* schedule around a new feud between Goldberg and Triple H over the coveted World Heavyweight Championship. Ultimately, this rivalry only existed so that Triple H could be the one to deal Goldberg his first WWE defeat.

WWE VS. JACKASS

Jackass and WWE. Seems like a natural partnership, doesn't it? WWE seem to think so, having teamed up with Jackass creator Jeff Tremaine for a WWE Network original series called *Swerved*. That was not the first time, however, that WWE and Jackass had been involved with one another.

Jackass stars Chris Pontius and Steve-O showed up on the October 16, 2006 edition of *Raw*. The Wildboyz ran into the 'Samoan Bulldozer', Umaga, who gave them a serious beat-down. Unfortunately, Steve-O didn't get the memo about selling Umaga's offence and began laughing at Pontius and trying to get up off the mat. In response the big man made sure to go back and dish out a few more extra-stiff strikes to keep him down.

It was an ugly episode, but not ugly enough to stop the two camps doing business together again in the summer of 2007. The cast of Jackass were supposed to resume their feud with Umaga, leading to a blowoff match at *SummerSlam '07*, which, incredibly, the Jackass gang were supposed to win. The posters were made and commercials filmed, and it was planned that the Jackass crew would cost Umaga his Intercontinental Championship in his match with Jeff Hardy at *The Great American Bash* to set it up.

However, following the Chris Benoit double-murder and suicide in June 2007, the Jackass gang wanted nothing to do with WWE and began to pull out of the deal, with show lead Johnny Knoxville specifically stating that he didn't want to be associated with WWE because of the Benoit tragedy.

The whole thing, which had been orchestrated by Shane McMahon, fell apart quickly once Knoxville pulled out, perhaps for the best as far as Umaga's career was concerned.

STING VS. STEVE AUSTIN

"I had been negotiating with Vince [McMahon], and one of the ideas was for me to debut at the end of WrestleMania XIX and confront 'Stone Cold' Steve Austin. Negotiations fell apart and it never happened, but it makes you wonder, 'What if?' That was one of the times I was talking with Vince, and it would've been an incredible night that would've translated into some major, major rivalries and match-ups for years to come." - Sting

Steve Austin admitted that he had no idea Sting was close to signing at that point, but agrees it would have been a moment for the ages and it's too bad it never happened. Austin and Sting had already worked together quite a bit in WCW in the early 90s when Sting was a top babyface and Austin was a rookie heel on the rise, and they had good chemistry together. While Sting may have been forty-four years old come WrestleMania XIX, history has proven he could still work to a high level into his fifties. There's no question that he could have done well in WWE and a match with Austin would have been a spectacle for the ages.

After Hulk Hogan dropped the WWF Title to Yokozuna at *King of the Ring '93*, WWE still had plans to use him going forward. Ultimately, all he ended up doing was a sparsely-attended European tour, but there were plans in motion at one stage for him to work a program with another of the WWF's resident goliaths, the 7'7" Giant Gonzalez. They even had a long-since forgotten stare-down designed to build anticipation for it.

Gonzalez has the distinction of being the only man in Undertaker's incredible *WrestleMania* Streak not to lose via pinfall or submission to the 'Dead Man', with his defeat at *WrestleMania IX* coming via disqualification as a means to protect him, keeping him relevant for a series down the line with Hogan.

The plan initially was for a series towards the end of the year at *Survivor Series*, with Hogan set to defend and lose his title to Bret Hart at *SummerSlam* first, but when that was changed the Hogan-Gonzalez bout was moved forward to the annual summer extravaganza.

It was typical Vince McMahon booking. The classic underdog Hulkster against an unstoppable giant dynamic that had worked so well in the 80's. It was a booking trope the WWF believed would work again to build Hogan back to his pre-steroid controversy levels.

In their angle shot two days after *King of the Ring*, Giant Gonzalez was brought out as an enforcer for Money Incorporated in a tag team match against Hogan and his chum Brutus Beefcake. Following the contest and a post-match brawl featuring among others The Smoking Gunns, Hogan and Gonzalez were left alone in the ring to face off. The giant retreated before they got physical, giving fans in the arena a tease of what was to come.

A few weeks later the Hogan-McMahon relationship broke down irreparably, so Hogan decided to leave the WWF, this time for good. By now McMahon was fed up of Gonzalez and his stilted performances, so he jobbed him out to The Undertaker at *SummerSlam*. That was the beginning of the end for the 7-foot monster, who after a blink-and-you-miss-it aborted babyface turn, left the company in October.

HULK HOGAN VS. GIANT GONZALEZ

RICK STEINER VS. RIC FLAIR

Before forming a renowned tag team with his brother Scott (who would later eclipse him in stature and become WCW World Heavyweight Champion), Rick Steiner played a nice-but-dim babyface character in the National Wrestling Alliance. And he was over, too. For a while in late 1988, Steiner was one of the most popular wrestlers the NWA had to offer. But under his amiable kayfabed exterior, Steiner was a serious dude, a college standout in amateur wrestling and a noted hard man in the dressing room.

Meanwhile, behind the scenes, booker Dusty Rhodes and World Champion Ric Flair were at loggerheads. The 'American Dream' had reached a point where he simply wanted the 'Nature Boy' gone, out of the title scene and preferably out of the company. With his Four Horsemen stablemates Arn Anderson and Tully Blanchard enjoying a new lease of life in the WWF as the Brain Busters, Flair no longer had the political back-up he was used to and found himself warring with Rhodes over every finish. Flair was scheduled to face Lex Luger at *Starrcade '88*, and as usual he and Rhodes couldn't agree on a finish. Things were getting nasty, and by this point it was the ultimate showdown. Whoever got his way this time would likely see the other man out of the promotion.

Rhodes came up with a classic old school solution to the issue: he would have Rick Steiner take the title from Flair at *Starrcade '88* instead of Luger. Not only that, but he would do it in a six-minute match inside of a steel cage. The idea was that Flair would have three options:

1. Turn up, do the job and lose the title as ordered in a humiliating fashion
2. Turn up, try to go into business for himself, and have hard-man Steiner forcibly pin him in an even more humiliating scene;
3. Simply quit, take his ball and go home.

Any one of those options suited Rhodes down to the ground.

But he'd reckoned without Jim Herd, who'd recently risen to the position of WCW Executive Vice President. Herd knew nothing about professional wrestling, having come from a position as regional manager of Pizza Hut. Panicked at the politicking surrounding him, he sought outside advice and was told that finishing the programme between Flair and Luger at *Starrcade* was the right direction to go... And that Flair needed to win.

Herd overruled Rhodes, and that's exactly how WCW's biggest night of the year finished, with Flair defeating Luger after a half hour big fight main event: cheating to win, naturally. Rhodes would be out of a job and out of WCW not long afterwards. Had Herd bowed to Rhodes' dubious wisdom, the outcome could have been significantly different. Steiner would probably have very quickly transitioned the belt to Luger following his win, while Flair would have likely abandoned the NWA for the WWF in 1988 instead of 1991, forming a Four Horsemen reunion under the WWF banner.

More than that, if he'd had his way Dusty Rhodes might have stayed with the NWA, cementing his political position, retaining the book and removing the need for the reshuffles that eventually got a certain young Eric Bischoff the top job in the company in 1993. There would have been no Monday Night War, no Attitude Era, no 'Stone Cold' Steve Austin. Nothing about the wrestling landscape that followed would have been the same.

26

BRET HART VS. HULK HOGAN

With his image tarnished due to allegations of steroid use following a disastrous appearance on The Arsenio Hall Show, Hulk Hogan stepped away from the spotlight in 1992 in order to let the heat surrounding him die down. When he returned the following year he was still undoubtedly the biggest star in the WWF, but his aura had significantly diminished. Vince McMahon saw Hogan as almost the antithesis of what he wanted the future of the WWF to be, with his focus firmly on pushing new, younger stars.

One of those stars was Bret Hart. The popular 'Hitman' was WWF Champion until WrestleMania IX where he was defeated by Yokozuna. Seconds later, Hogan waltzed to the ring and scooped up all of Hart's heat, challenging Yokozuna to an impromptu match and beating him in record time to lift his fifth WWF Championship. Hart was soothed with the knowledge that his loss was only fleeting, because McMahon had promised he would get the belt back at SummerSlam '93, where Hogan would put him over for the title. Hogan even told Hart after the WrestleMania match, "Thank you brother. I won't forget it. I'll be happy to return the favour."

Hogan passing the torch would be a significant moment for Hart that helped legitimise him as the new leader of the WWF. To get him ready for such a monumental victory Hart needed to be built up strongly first, a feat McMahon intended to achieve by having him win the inaugural King of the Ring pay-per-view. Hogan and Hart shot some promotional photos designed to build the SummerSlam match, and the bout was set.

However, Hogan had other ideas. He balked at the prospect of putting over the much smaller Hart and refused to do the match. His return had been a flop. He was receiving negative reactions around the country and it had dawned on him that he was going to be jeered at SummerSlam against the now far more-popular Hart. So Hogan backed out, telling McMahon that Hart was not in his league. The decision was made to have Yokozuna beat Hogan instead, giving him his second run with the title.

When Hart learned what Hogan had said he was livid and confronted him backstage at King of the Ring just prior to going out for his tournament final match with Bam Bam Bigelow. Hart reminded Hogan what he had told him after WrestleMania and then told him in no uncertain terms what he thought of him. Hogan was almost speechless, only managing to mutter something about Hart not having the full story. The next day Hogan confirmed that Hart beating him had been the plan and it was Vince who had changed it, not him. They all met in Vince's office, where McMahon denied ever having said the match would be for the title, despite the photos that had been shot with the belt very much a focus providing evidence to the contrary.

Hogan left the WWF soon after that and did not return until 2002, by which point Hart had retired. They crossed paths briefly in WCW and worked a handful of house show matches and a short, truncated affair on Nitro, but that was it. That aside, the bigtime Hogan-Hart dream match that many hoped for never transpired.

MORDECAI VS. THE UNDERTAKER

Between 2002 and 2004, vampire-lover Kevin Fertig wrestled in WWE developmental group OVW as Seven, a gimmick based on the seven deadly sins (An identical gimmick to one attempted in 1999 by Dustin Runnels in WCW). Then he received a call from WWE creative telling him he was being brought up to the main roster. The gimmick he would be portraying was Mordecai—a name taken from the Hebrew Bible—but the look and persona was actually inspired by Scottish grappler Peter 'Conscience' Murphy, who had trained with Fertig in OVW. With WWE liking the gimmick but not offering Murphy a contract, they decided to steal the look and give it to Fertig.

Mordecai was a religious zealot character who dressed in all-white (complete with bleached white hair and beard), carried an oversized sword, and promised he would rid the world of sin. Vignettes aired hyping his debut, which eventually came at *Judgement Day '04* in a 3-minute destruction of Scotty 2 Hotty. Mordecai had a memorable entrance and a striking gimmick, but in the ring he was nothing special and the fans did not take to him.

It was no coincidence that Mordecai's gimmick was very similar to that of company franchise The Undertaker. Fertig was essentially playing the same role only dressed in white rather than black. Indeed, that was the point. Mordecai was being groomed for a headline feud with 'Taker later in the year.

But it didn't quite work out. Mordecai was history within a couple of weeks, leaving WWE seeking an alternative to work with Undertaker. They opted for the bumbling John Heidenreich in his place, which ended up being an even worse idea.

JUSTIN BIEBER, BIG SHOW & JOHN CENA VS. THE WYATTS

In what might well be one of the craziest pitches in WWE history, Justin Bieber was considered for involvement in a match at *SummerSlam '14*. According to former WWE writer Kevin Eck:

"The idea was that Bieber would team with John Cena and Big Show to face the Wyatt Family in a six-man tag match that would have headlined SummerSlam in Los Angeles.

"The proposed match was discussed among the booking team (which I was on) about five months before SummerSlam, but a deal with Bieber never came to fruition. I'm not sure how close it was to actually happening."

Quite rightly, Eck had expressed concerns that aligning Cena with Bieber wouldn't have done the grappler any favours at that time, considering the pop star's various controversies.

"To address that concern, the creative suggestion was that Cena would become increasingly annoyed by Bieber in the weeks leading up to the match, but Big Show, who would be portrayed as Bieber's friend, would repeatedly play peacemaker.

"After the babyfaces went over in the match, Bieber would be so obnoxious in trying to take credit for the win that Cena would hit the Attitude Adjustment on him for a big pop."

PAUL HEYMAN VS. PAUL BEARER

At *WrestleMania 29* The Undertaker came out of his annual hibernation to battle C.M. Punk. The original plan to build up the contest was for Undertaker to counter Punk's mouthy manager Paul Heyman by bringing back his long-time sidekick Paul Bearer. At one stage plans for Heyman and Bearer to get into a physical altercation were on the table, but sadly, things took a tragic turn one month prior to the show when Bearer passed away. In a classless move, WWE used Bearer' death to promote the match, having Heyman dress up as the deceased manager while C.M. Punk openly mocked his death, crossing a line in the eyes of most observers.

DANA WHITE VS. VINCE MCMAHON

Business was hardly booming for WWE in 2010, so looking for a hook to sell *WrestleMania XXVII*, Vince McMahon reached out to UFC owner Dana White in an attempt to secure a deal for Brock Lesnar to appear on the annual extravaganza. UFC was red hot at the time and Lesnar was the group's biggest star, so it made sense from a business perspective for McMahon to try for him.

Lesnar was keen on the idea and shot an angle with potential 'Mania opponent The Undertaker at UFC 121, unbeknownst to White. But when McMahon called White to talk terms, the UFC promoter told him there was no way he was letting his biggest drawing fighter step back into the wrestling ring while he was still promoting his real fights.

Undeterred, McMahon instead suggested that he and White step into the squared circle and work a wrestling match on WWE's biggest show of the year. Suspecting White may not be keen on a worked contest, he told the baffled UFC chief that if that did not appeal to him, he was willing to fight him for real. McMahon was 65-years-old at the time and White was in his early 40s, but McMahon firmly believed he could fight him and that he could win.

Others did too, including boxing legend Mike Tyson who upon being asked who would win a fight between the two promoting heavyweights declared, "Oh, that's a tough one because Vince is pretty big and tough and he's got the wrestling moves down. Let's stick with Vince in that one.

UFC star Chael Sonnen had an alternative viewpoint, commenting, "Vince would be so punch drunk against Dana, even his straight edge champion C.M. Punk would feel tipsy."

White was unequivocal in his response to the challenge. "I laughed and said, 'You're crazy, you're out of your mind,'" said White. "I told Vince he was too old. That we were both too old, for the record. I'm younger than him by 20 years but I'm a beat up 43-year-old man."

McMahon did not get Lesnar or White, so instead he turned to Dwayne 'The Rock' Johnson to save *WrestleMania* from bombing. Rock's involvement with WWE helped turn the company's ailing PPV business around, so it turned out to be a better option anyway.

BRET HART VS. SHAWN MICHAELS

During a meeting with Jim Ross and Vince McMahon in his Calgary home in the fall of 1996 while discussing terms on his re-signing with the WWF, Bret Hart first pitched a series of matches with Shawn Michaels. The first was to take place at *WrestleMania 13* and would see Hart go over Michaels for the WWF Championship, a returned favour from Hart's job to Shawn at *WrestleMania XII*. That would even the pair at 1-1 on pay-per-view, setting the stage for a rubber match that Hart was more than happy to put Michaels over in, passing the torch to him as the future of the WWF.

In a curious bit of happenstance, on the flight back home to Calgary, Hart ended up seated next to Michaels. After amiably comparing notes about professional and work lives, Hart let slip the details of the angle he'd just laid before McMahon, noting that it would conclude with Michaels winning the tie-breaker at some undetermined point down the line. Michaels, for his part, didn't express much joy at the idea, instead getting hung up on the crux of the second match, where he would return Hart's job from *WrestleMania XII*.

"I saw the colour drain from his face," said Hart, when he informed Michaels of how the first return bout would conclude. "He clearly didn't like the sound of any of this."

Despite Michaels' obvious discomfort at being asked to lay down at *WrestleMania 13* with months of advance notice, Hart mostly dismissed it. After all, Michaels would reign supreme in the end anyway—what was one pothole on the road to immortality?

Eight months later on the night of a special Thursday edition of *Raw* titled *Thursday Raw Thursday*, the pothole was filled to its brim by flash flooding. Ten days earlier, Hart engaged in a tense phone call with McMahon, where he was stunned to learn that his highly-anticipated rematch with Michaels at *WrestleMania* would not have the WWF Championship at stake. Instead, the new plan was that Michaels would drop the belt on the Thursday special to Sycho Sid, where scornful Hart would run interference. Three nights later at *In Your House: Final Four*, Michaels would then prevent Hart from winning the *Royal Rumble* restart match, leaving The Undertaker as lone survivor to challenge for Sid's gold.

"It's too predictable now. I'm changing it," McMahon told Hart of the title match plans when pressed for information. McMahon went so far as to suggest that Hart's match with Michaels would be a ladder match in which Michaels would put his hair on the line and would subsequently be shaved bald in defeat. For Hart, juvenile public humiliation at the expense of his professional rival was a lousy stand-in for an epic showdown with the WWF Title up for grabs. With Hart earning $1.5 million per year for the next three years from a company that wasn't in its most solvent times, the *WrestleMania* demotion seemed counterproductive to him.

In the end, Hart didn't get any match with Michaels, belt or no belt, no ladder to climb, and no hair to shave. Dropping the belt back to the unreliable, lumbering Sid en route to an even more high-profile loss to Hart at *WrestleMania* was the sort of one-two wallop that Michaels had no interest in enduring. At his wit's end from a fracturing body, the pressures of being the face of the promotion, and a loss of seventy-five percent of his Kliq co-conspirators to WCW, Michaels dropped a bomb on the WWF office: he was handing in the WWF Championship belt, and removing himself from the ring for the foreseeable future.

That led to Shawn's infamous "lost my smile" promo on *Thursday Raw Thursday*, not to mention a complete rejigging of the *WrestleMania 13* card. Hart would now be working with Steve Austin, a continuation of a feud that had been rumbling since *Survivor Series* in November. The match blew the roof off the building and is considered among the finest matches in *WrestleMania* and indeed WWE history, so it likely worked out better in the end than a Michaels-Hart bout would have. In addition to putting on a classic, the Hart-Austin match was really responsible for "making" 'Stone Cold' Steve Austin, with the WWF turning him babyface and allowing the masses to embrace him as an antihero.

Michaels returned to the ring a few weeks after 'Mania, with his "career-ending" knee injury redefining the word career to mean "a couple of months", causing a sceptical Hart to swear blind that the only reason he pulled out of *WrestleMania* was to avoid doing the return job he owed him.

FEATURE:

BY GEORGE J. RUTHERFORD

10 THINGS YOU LEARN AS A WWE CREATIVE WRITER

Even in the post-Kayfabe, "Total Divas" era, much of what happens behind the scenes at World Wrestling Entertainment is still very much a mystery to the general populous. It's important for super fans to know that the "reality" of what we see is still very much controlled by the powers-that-be in Titan Tower.

In 2007, a combination of tenacity, good timing and dumb luck landed this contributing author a job of which most could only dream. I had the nerve wracking pleasure of being interviewed (four times) and ultimately hired by Vince McMahon to be a creative writer for the SmackDown brand of the WWE.

For those who are unfamiliar, the creative team at WWE is completely integrated into the production of television and pay-per-view events. We were on the road 300 days of the year, right alongside the talent. We are in the arenas, the planes and the hotels.

We see the good, the bad and the sometimes very ugly. While the average tenure as a creative team member isn't typically very long (Mine certainly wasn't), there is a lot to be learned about the inner workings of one of the craziest businesses in the world.

Be advised: This isn't a "dirt sheet" about "Who hated who" or "Who was using performance enhancing substances". Those are out there if that's your thing. This is a list of what I think are interesting facts that you pick up in a day in the life of a proverbial fly on WWE's grandiose wall.

It's Scripted… But Not As Much As You Think

Everyone over the age of 10 knows that, in professional wrestling, the match results are pre-determined. Contrary to popular belief, the writers don't actually write the matches: that is done by "producers" or "road agents". They work with the talent to create the best match possible based on the story lines developed by the creative team.

The best laid plans, however, often fall to ruin. Whether it's an unexpected injury, a delayed flight, personal issues or just good old backstage politics, the scripted plan would sometimes have to be changed at the zero hour!

In one instance, due to a travel conflict, we had to completely change a match, rewrite the script, distribute it, get the talent together with a producer, and come up with a full match less than 90 minutes before going on live TV. What makes the guys in the ring professional is that they were able to pull it off as though it were the plan all along.

Obviously not every match is a classic, but sometimes the wrestlers are asked to overcome some pretty serious hindrances and make it look natural like Butch Reed. It's for this reason that many lower and mid-card talent travel with the TV crew, even if they aren't scheduled to appear. You never know when you will get called in to take over a main event.

Vince Was Very Particular About His Snacks

Before any TV or pay-per-view event, Vince and certain members of the production team would meet early in the day to have what is called a "Production Meeting".

These meetings covered everything from script changes and talent issues to where we could find worms for "The Boogeyman" to eat in the ring. While it was likely that twelve things would change by show time, the production meeting was important in establishing a baseline for the day.

One of the well-known rules of WWE production meetings was that there was to always be a Detour protein bar and a Diet Dr. Pepper at Vince's seat for the meeting. Oftentimes it would be the responsibility of Writer Assistants to procure these items and be sure they were in place before Vince's arrival. He didn't go crazy about it. The bar didn't have to be a specific flavour and the Diet Dr. Pepper didn't have to be exactly 47.2 degrees or anything. That's just what he liked to snack on.

Mr. McMahon is definitely one of those people who becomes so busy that he forgets to eat. When this happened, there would always be a spare Detour bar and Diet Dr. Pepper laying around that needed to be discarded after the meeting. Needless to say, I ended up consuming a few Detours and Peppers during that time.

Mark Henry Has A Great Sense Of Humour

Once, before a TV taping, I was ringside watching match rehearsals. I was reviewing the script and observing how the guys in the ring were executing the plan for TV that night. My focus was snapped as I felt a giant man-paw clap onto my shoulder. When I turned my head, I was staring into the very intense face of "The World's Strongest Man", Mark Henry.

Mark gripped my shoulder and leaned in closer. Still not breaking eye contact, he growled:

"Who are you?"

"Um, hi Mark. I'm George. I'm the new writer for SmackDown".

Leaning in even closer, he whispered, "Do you like men, George?"

At this point, my brain flipped through every possible response to this question. For some inexplicable reason, my better sense settled on, "Um, not in the romantic sense Mark".

Letting out a long exhale, he replied, "Oh, you will…"

Allowing a terribly awkward beat, he stood up, his face then pulling back into a perfectly pleasant smile as he said, "Aw man, I'm just f*ck*in' with you. Welcome to the show!"

In every encounter after that, Mark was awesome to talk with and had a great sense of humour. What else do you expect from the guy who convincingly pulled off the "Sexual Chocolate" persona?

John Cena Is A True Babyface

One doesn't have to look far to find an example of John Cena using his powers for good. Whether it's a Make-A-Wish visit or a simple autograph signing, Cena has truly established himself as a face of the WWE.

If your sceptical side leads you to believe that it's all just good PR for the company, I have a little slice of life story that suggest otherwise.

Being a native Pennsylvanian, I was thrilled when my father and sister were able to attend a show in State College. Backstage, they were taking in the controlled chaos that was life in the WWE. My sister timidly asked if she would be able to meet John Cena.

Now, nobody is busier behind the scenes than Cena. There is a large premium put upon his time. I managed to find him backstage (in an interview, naturally). As soon as there was a break, I asked him if he could take a second to meet my family. He immediately stopped what he was doing and followed me to them.

John spent several minutes chatting with my dad and sister. He didn't come off as rushed or inconvenienced. He stayed longer than he needed to and made them feel like the most important people in the arena.

From what I saw, the guy was always a true babyface.

You Get Pitched A Ton Of Bad Ideas

As a creative team member, it's common for your phone to ring with pitches from wrestlers who either aren't on the main roster or who are unhappy with their current character. In the interest of self-preservation, lower and mid-card talent will pitch a ton of ideas to the creative team in hopes of becoming the next breakout superstar. Some of these ideas are pretty good and can be developed into characters. Others, not so much.

Sometimes, ideas were pitched about storylines or specific match ideas. They weren't all winners. Keep in mind, ideas that made the cut at this time included Paul Burchill being both a pirate and ambiguously incestuous, Eugene being developmentally disabled and the somewhat racist "Cryme Tyme" gimmick.

That being said, imagine the pitched ideas that never made it further than a phone call. Here's a couple: Domino (Of the "Deuce and Domino" tag team) as a street-wise gangster rapper persona with a skinny white guy manager. From "Happy Days" to "Boyz n The Hood"? Nah.

Some may have read about this in interviews, but I remember when the idea was first floated of calling Mark Henry "The Silverback". I recall shrinking in my chair at that one. I did support Melina's movie star gimmick though, because I got to be one of the paparazzi who followed her to the ring... Amazing.

Nobody Messes With The Undertaker

Behind the scenes, different Superstars have various levels of sway. "Curtain Jerkers" and mid-card talent were mostly at the mercy of the creative team when it came to character and storyline development. Main eventers were obviously given more consideration. Guys like Triple H and Shawn Michaels even participated in the production meetings. That being said, nobody on the roster had more political clout than the Deadman.

When Undertaker was involved in a storyline, we would be sure to call and consult with him before any decisions were made. Not because he demanded it, but because he just earned that level of credibility.

It wasn't just with the creative team that Undertaker's word was law. He served, and likely still serves, as an unofficial judge and jury when it came to backstage drama between talent. 'Taker would hear all sides of an argument, and hand down his decision (which was always ultimately about the greater good, and everyone knew it).

By all accounts, Undertaker is a fair and just field General who never abuses his position. He keeps the peace and expects a certain level of respect and professionalism from everyone around him. While Vince is always the true final word, Undertaker is the man in the locker room.

There Is An Awesome "Merch Vault" In Titan Tower

In WWE's "Titan Tower" headquarters in Stamford, CT, there is a room. Available to employees only, this ordinary-looking office space is, in fact, an awesome merch vault. During my first week on the job, an HR guy took me for a tour of the building. There was a fantastic gym, a top-notch cafeteria and classic memorabilia (Like Andre the Giant's boot) on display on every floor.

The gem of this tour, undoubtedly, was the merch vault. Rows and rows of every type of WWE merchandise one can imagine. DVDs, posters, championship belts, shirt, action figures and giant foam hands lined the walls and shelves. For a child of the '80s, I was thrilled to see how much classic merch was there. The vintage rubber action figures, trading cards and old championship belt replicas took me right back to being seven years old.

Like a kid in a candy store, I was given the opportunity to search the piles of treasure for anything I wanted to take with me. Fighting my initial instinct to stuff my pockets and run out with my arms loaded, I chose a few choice DVD sets, made a mental picture of the room, and exited with my professionalism intact.

JBL Is Not Easily Impressed

To say the least, JBL has presence. When he walks into a room, or building, everyone knows it. He is a large man with a booming voice. He also has no qualms about letting people know what he thinks. This includes letting new writers know what he thinks of their chances for success in the company.

When new creative members, as I was, met JBL for the first time, there was apparently a customary ritual involved. When I introduced myself to Mr. Layfield and shook his hand, he immediately gave me the name "D*ckh**d #16" and took a picture of me with his phone. This name and picture were then put into his phone along with the names and pictures of D*ckh**ds number one through fifteen.

Once I was officially part of the menagerie, JBL informed me (and everyone) that the over/under on me lasting in the company was two weeks. I'm not sure if any real money was placed on these bets, or if it was just amusing to him, but at that moment it became my goal in life to last at least fifteen days.

Determined to show JBL that I had the grit to make it in the dog-eat-dog world of Sports Entertainment, I tracked him down after the two-week mark and informed him that I had beaten his two-week prediction. JBL waited about half a beat, said "Good job D*ckh**d 16" and went on about his day.

There Is A Reason SmackDown Is Not Live

In 2007, RAW was shot live on Monday nights. It was the flagship show and, for the most part, touted the top talent in the company. SmackDown's top talent consisted of more kid-friendly gimmicks and veterans who were being utilized to develop lower level wrestlers.

SmackDown was taped on Tuesdays, edited, and aired on Fridays. From what I observed, it was a good call to not have SmackDown go directly to the viewing audience. For one, some of the more high-flying talent were on the SmackDown roster. Even top guys like Rey Mysterio didn't always look as smooth live as he did on edited TV. For this reason, many of these matches were "cleaned up" in post-production to make the televised product look as polished as possible.

Once, there was a match so...let's say unpolished, that it was just eliminated from the show. It was Chavo Guerrero vs. Jimmy Wang Yang. Both very talented, high risk performers. For whatever reason, the choreography just wasn't working that night. The crowd were quickly turning on them, and I was fortunate enough to be out on the floor to see the match. As I watched the bout, I tried to figure out how the editors were going to string together a tight show out of this display. As it came to be, they couldn't figure it out either and cut it completely.

Dusty Rhodes Deserves His Legendary Status

During my tenure, Dusty Rhodes was the head writer of ECW. This gave me the chance to sit with him in the writer's room and pick his brain about all things wrestling. His decades of insight into programming, story building, and the art of "putting butts in seats" was invaluable to someone as green as me. In the creative process, I never once saw Dusty push his own agenda or insert himself into the spotlight for no reason. He was, however, always willing to jump in and do what was needed for the good of the show.

One day, I had the rare occasion to enjoy a lengthy one-on-one discussion with Dusty. When I asked him about the difference between the business now (now meaning 2007) and the old days, Dusty looked me in the eye and told me:

"Let me tell ya somethin' young fella'. The difference is that ever since Vincent Mac-Mahon went on television and had to tell the world that wrasslin' was scripted...there was no goin' back afta' that!"

Essentially, Dusty explained that matches couldn't have long, low periods like they did pre-attitude era. They needed more excitement, but we still had to protect the talent from too much danger and focus on better storylines to build drama. Always one to put the team first and take care of everyone, "The American Dream" was a real class act.

REBRANDING

HOW DIFFERENT SOME GIMMICKS COULD HAVE BEEN...

CHILLY MCFREEZE

Fed up of being asked to portray The Ringmaster, a voiceless character with no personality, Steve Austin took stock of his lot and demanded a change in the way he was presented: 'Stone Cold' Steve Austin.

Frustrated with his dead-end, ill-fitting gimmick, Austin pulled Vince McMahon aside during a television taping and requested that he be given the chance to come up with a different ring name and a fresh persona for himself. He told McMahon matter-of-factly, "Vince, I'm not The Ringmaster. I'm just not feeling it." McMahon dismissed the notion, telling Austin that he was a master of what he did in the ring, thus it was only logical that he was The Ringmaster. Usually a midcard talent like Austin would be wise to not talk back to McMahon, but Austin was not happy in the WWF and was more than prepared to leave the company in search of creative satisfaction if it came to it.

Plus, he already had an idea in mind having just watched an inspiring documentary about serial killer 'The Iceman' Richard Kulinski. Austin wanted his WWF persona to be reborn as a similarly bald, bearded, ruthless, cold-hearted killer type, and he pitched the idea to Vince. Admiring Austin's determination, McMahon agreed to consider the request. "We'll give it some thought and maybe we'll come up with something else," he told him.

Austin was dismayed when the WWF's creative team came back to him a few days later with a list of potential names that had missed the point entirely. They had misinterpreted the request for references to 'The Iceman', believing Austin wanted temperature-based monikers. Suggestions included Fang McFrost, Ice Dagger, Austin's personal favourite Otto von Ruthless, and the least appropriate of all, Chilly McFreeze. Every single one of the names handed to him was considerably worse than his current Ringmaster moniker.

Jim Cornette sheds some light on where the wildly inappropriate names originated: "Those names came from a department in the WWF called Creative Services. Whenever you would sit around a table with Vince and get ideas for new talent he would ask for Creative Services to come up with names for them based on what their M.O. was going to be. So if a guy was going to be a plumber, then they would write down names based on plumbers, which is where something like T.L. Hopper came from. Vince would get ideas for outfits and tell Creative Services to design him something that looked like the vision in his head. But they weren't wrestling people, they were trained monkeys."

Seemingly on an entirely different wavelength to the people tasked with driving his stalling career, Austin grumbled about the situation to his English wife Jeanie. He admitted to being at his wits end, unable to bear the thought of having to go back to the office with no alternative to the names he had so vehemently shot down. As Austin paced around his Texas home struggling to come up with something, he began contemplating how he would go about trying to make one of the inane ideas the WWF had presented him with work. Then Jeanie said something that changed not only his career, but ultimately the course of the entire wrestling industry.

"Steve, calm down and give it a rest for a while. Don't worry about it, you'll think of something. Now come on, drink your tea before it gets *stone cold*." Unwittingly, she had stumbled across the perfect nickname for a character that would soon capture the zeitgeist of a generation. 'Stone Cold' fit the description perfectly, it was *exactly* what Austin wanted... Even if the story behind it is a little wussy. Something about the beer-swilling redneck delicately sipping tea just doesn't sit right, perhaps because it conjures up images of Hulk Hogan wearing a tutu and sticking his pinkie finger out while enjoying the beverage in movie nightmare Mr. Nanny.

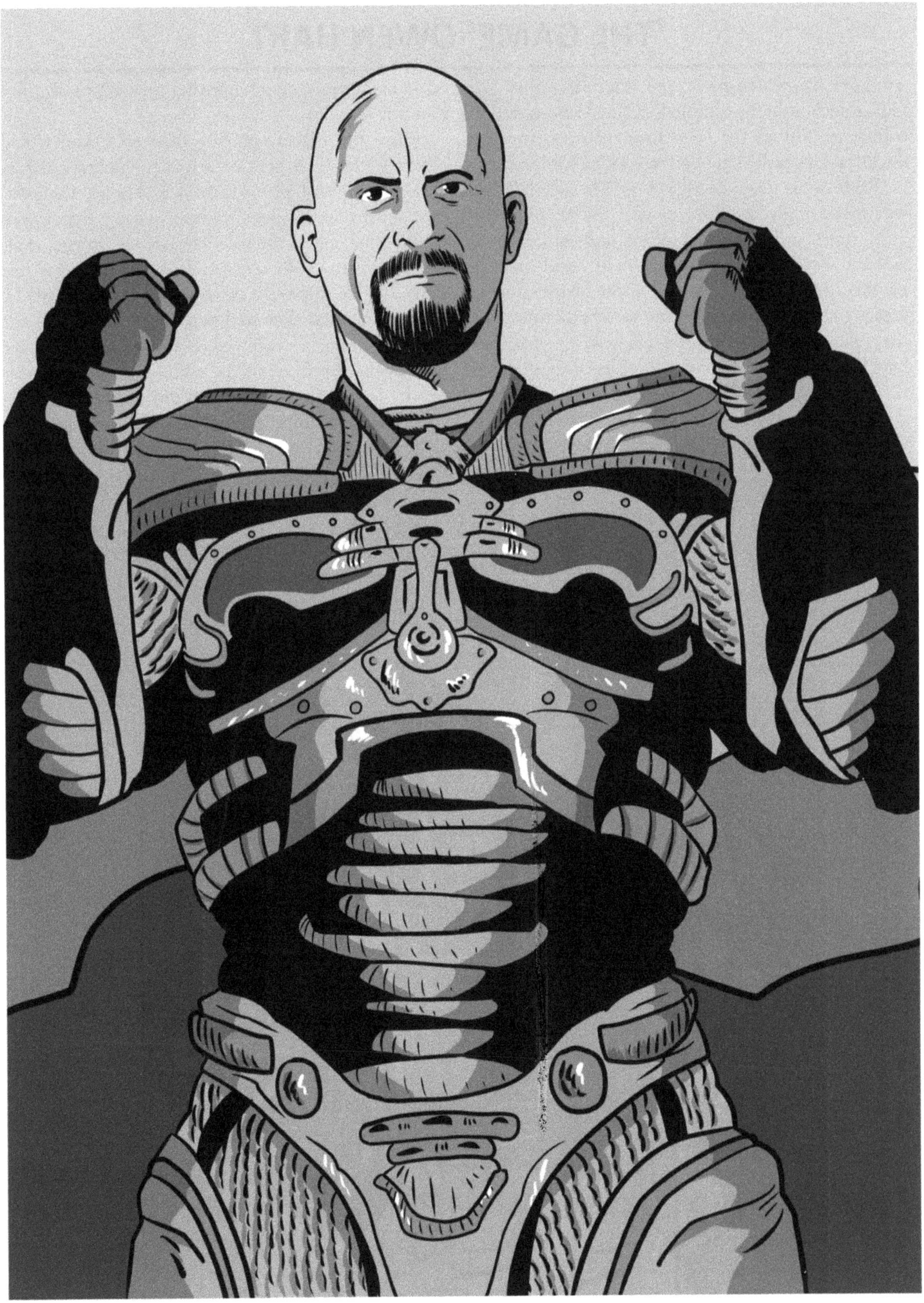

'THE GAME' OWEN HART

Triple H has stated in several interviews that 'The Game' nickname he adopted in 1999 was actually a tribute to honour the late Owen Hart, as the gimmick was originally intended as an idea for him.

Prior to his tragic death at *Over The Edge '99*, Hart was increasingly disgruntled with the WWF's shift away from professional wrestling and into raunchy, violent, lewd sports entertainment, and like his brother Bret he was not shy about expressing his feelings about it. Thinking they were placating Hart, they allowed him to reprise his role of superhero babyface The Blue Blazer, the voice of morality in the lawless WWF. Of course, Attitude Era fans hated him for censoring what they wanted to see, but that was the idea.

Once the Blazer run was finished Owen would revert to being a serious wrestler, rechristened as 'The Game' and promoted as a serious, thinking-man's wrestler. It goes without saying that Owen would have suited the role. He had the in-ring skills and charisma to do it justice. At the time, his mic skills also far surpassed those of the dreary Triple H. A more talented all-round performer, with the same push as Triple H received Owen could well have been at the forefront of the entire industry. Chances are the landscape of pro wrestling would have been very different had he lived to perform the role.

THE MILLIONAIRE'S CLUB AVENGERS

In 2000, Vince Russo and Eric Bischoff had a plan to help turn WCW's fortunes around. Both had spent some time away from the promotion, and upon reflection felt they had an ideal storyline to make the struggling product enjoyable again. The idea was pretty simple, but it would involve a lot of trust from those who had been on top for years.

Known as the Millionaire's Club, the likes of Hulk Hogan, DDP, and Kevin Nash were considered the ageing veterans of the company. Russo and Bischoff decreed that there needed to be more of an emphasis on youth if WCW was going to have a future, thus The New Blood was born to feud with the older stars.

The Millionaire Club vs. New Blood storyline did actually happen, but not as originally intended. When Vince Russo joined WCW in 1999 he immediately began the process of writing veteran stars such as Ric Flair and Hulk Hogan off television. Neither legend was particularly happy about it, but Russo's grand idea was that they'd return further down the road, repaired from the character damage both had suffered due to terrible booking over the past few years. Further to this, they'd both be part of an angle which actually shares striking similarities with 2012 superhero movie *The Avengers*.

In that film, Nick Fury leads a team of superheroes Iron Man, Hulk, Thor, Captain America, Hawkeye and Black Widow in a fight to save the world from the evil Loki, who is trying to destroy it. Over in WCW, Russo's plan was for Eric Bischoff to act in the Fury role, leading the likes of Hogan, Flair, Nash and others against the upstart New Blood who were trying to take over the world, or rather World Championship Wrestling, for good.

While much can be said about some of Russo's ideas (and many of them feature in this book), the fact is that this one remains a perfectly viable angle, and it's a shame it didn't happen. While fans did see the Millionaire's Club come to fruition, it wasn't handled in the same manner and was ultimately a washout. The booking was ineffective, which did not help, but most importantly the egos of the veterans stood in the way. With the majority having creative control to manage their own programs, Bischoff and Russo's hands were tied. Yet another promising WCW angle that was ultimately ruined by ego.

GEORGE W. BUSH

When Muhammad Hassan was dropped from television in 2004 due to fan backlash against his terrorist gimmick, his manager Daivari also disappeared. WWE were eager to find a new role for him elsewhere on the card and discussed potential gimmick ideas for his return.

It was Stephanie McMahon who called him into her office for a meeting to discuss the brilliant idea the creative team had come up with: they wanted to repackage him as George W. Bush... That's right, the American President at the time. Let thank sink in.

Actually, Daivari was not intended to be a facsimile of the controversial President, but rather he was share his name and become a caricature of American patriotism, dressed from head to toe in the star-spangled banner. After having feared for his life while playing his previous terrorist role, Daivari had no intention of heat baiting in the same way and turned the character down without hesitation.

Eventually, he'd return to manage Kurt Angle and do a spot of wrestling on occasion, but he was never given anything resembling a push. Turn down the McMahons when they present a gimmick and that is generally the way it goes.

MASON THE MUTILATOR

It might seem a small issue, but without a great name, Mick Foley's Mankind might have never achieved the cult appeal he did in WWE. He should thank himself lucky then, that he didn't accept Vince McMahon's initial suggestion. The chairman wanted Foley to replace his Cactus Jack character with the Hannibal Lecter-inspired masked man, but wanted to call him Mason the Mutilator. Foley, realising the name sucked, countered with Mankind the Mutilator, so he could do promos about the "evils of Mankind", giving his character a unique split-personality edge. McMahon agreed and his career was saved.

SPACE CORPS HOLLY

Other than a brief ill-advised stint as a racing car driving his early days, Hardcore Holly was a guy that never really seemed to have a true gimmick. Somewhat aping his real-life backstage demeanour, Holly was little more than a surly redneck, who hated everyone and liked to beat people up.

When *ECW On SyFy* debuted in the summer of 2006, the WWE creative department were told—as per the network's request—to come up with some ideas for gimmicks that had a supernatural/science-fiction slant to them. Former WWE writer Court Bauer admitted years later that he had pitched an outlandish idea for Hardcore Holly to go into outer space with a pet monkey.

Apparently the proposed plan included WWE announcing that they were working with NASA, then Holly would resurface after a short while, clad in an astronaut suit and accompanied to the ring by a pet monkey. Apparently then creative team head Stephanie McMahon was both amused and disturbed by the idea.

But, alas, Space Corps Holly never made it to air. It's hard to know how close it came to becoming a reality, but it sounds more like a joke that got out of hand. Bauer himself has said that it was just an idea that was thrown around for fun, but you never really know in WWE. The same was true of the infamous Billionaire Ted skits in 1996 and they made it to air.

MARK JINDRAK IN EVOLUTION

Oh how the history of wrestling could have been so different. It's hard to imagine anyone other than Triple H, Ric Flair, Randy Orton and Batista comprising Evolution, but 'The Animal' almost didn't make the cut.

Mark Jindrak, most famous for his poor tag team runs with Garrison Cade and Luther Reigns (and an even lamer 'Reflection of Perfection' solo gimmick) was the man whom WWE and, in particular, Triple H had initially wanted in the group. Triple H was trying to mentor Jindrak and Orton, both of whom WWE had high hopes for.

Unfortunately, both Jindrak and Orton were very immature at that point in their careers. They even staged a pretend fight in a bar, completely for their own amusement, after a house show one time. It was incidents like this that made WWE second guess the rookies' dedication to the cause.

WWE went so far as to shoot Evolution vignettes with Jindrak in them, but after viewing them back it was felt that something was off and the chemistry wasn't quite right. Jindrak just didn't give off the correct vibe or project that he belonged in a group of that stature. So he was switched out for Batista, who ended up becoming one of the biggest wrestling stars in the world.

HIROHITO

WWE aren't the best when it comes to racial sensitivity. Although they've tried to become better about it in recent years, there was a time when every racial stereotype was propagated in the name of cheap heat.

When it comes to Japanese wrestlers, especially, you could bet that WWE wouldn't give them gimmicks other than 'martial arts expert' or 'mysterious foreigner'. Still, those gimmicks are a thousand times better than what was proposed for Kenzo Suzuki before his WWE debut in spring 2004.

WWE originally wanted the bumbling Suzuki to play a character named Hirohito, grandson of the famous Japanese World War II Emperor. WWE even aired vignettes for the character on *Raw* but quickly pulled them when they realised (or were warned) that it would cause serious heat in Japan, a country that WWE intended to further expand into.

Amazingly, Suzuki as Hirohito was going to be brought in as a main event player to feud with Chris Jericho and Chris Benoit in a United States versus Japan angle. Wait, weren't Y2J and Benoit Canadian? They were, which is exactly why WWE changed their hometowns to 'Manhasset, New York' and 'Atlanta, Georgia' respectively. All to feud with Suzuki, of all people!

'PROFESSOR X' HADE VANSEN

Much like Dustin Runnels' cancelled Seven gimmick in WCW and the awful in-joke Kizarny, WWE were clearly keen on the idea of investing in Hade Vansen given the money and time they spent on promos hyping his arrival.

The British wrestler was signed to a deal in 2007 before a knee injury sidelined him for a year. That could have been the end for him, but instead he was picked up as for an intriguing looking gimmick that would see him feud with The Undertaker.

In the promos—which ran for two weeks—Vansen talked about "the darkness" (probably not the band) and threw in lots of other "dark" references to promote his suitability to fight the 'Dead Man'. The segments were all written by Buffy's husband and one-time WWE writer Freddie Prinze Jnr, who was apparently stoked about the idea.

According to Vansen, he would have been the head of a stable seeking to dethrone 'Taker: "I was going to lead a gang of X-Men style mutants. Every week, I would send one of these guys after The Undertaker. After he had beaten them all, he would eventually face me at *WrestleMania XXV*."

Sadly, though, the gimmick was dropped mysteriously and Vansen was let go without getting his chance. His suspicions as to why sound believable:

"Nobody ever gave me a reason why I'd been released, but there is one story that keeps doing the rounds, and I don't know if this is true or not, and that is Vince McMahon saw me backstage and thought I was way too small to be hanging with The Undertaker."

Once again, in Vince McMahon's world, size really is everything.

NAKED GOLDUST

In 1995, the World Wrestling Federation was struggling and lacking depth, so McMahon responded by creating the intentionally shocking and controversy-baiting androgyne known as Goldust. To this day the original incarnation of the character that saw portrayer Dustin Runnels perform the role of a vicious sexual predator, remains one of the most controversial characters in wrestling history. Some on the roster found the homoerotic overtones a little too much to bear, with Scott Hall in particular uncomfortable working with Goldust because of the awkward questions it would lead to from his kids.

As the years rolled on, the character evolved due to outside pressures from gay rights groups. The Hollywood origins introduced at the start were largely phased out and Goldust became a far more standard pro wrestler. But as the character became less controversial it also became less effective, so in 1997, Runnels turned Goldust into TAFKA Goldust, a role that saw him dress as everyone from Marilyn Manson through to a new-born baby.

That was a step too far and fans rejected the gimmick for becoming too outlandish. Back at the drawing board the WWF creative bods came up with another idea: Goldust, an obviously voyeuristic character, could become a streaker. After all, he had already appeared on television wearing thongs and other assorted women's underwear, so it was hardly much of a leap.

Instead Runnels left the WWF and the gimmick remained on the shelf for a while before eventually being handed to former Arkansas pig farmer and lower card struggler Dennis 'Phineas Godwinn' Knight. Knight was rebranded as Naked Mideon, a mostly-nude grappler who competed with nothing more than a small flap covering his privates. Dustin Runnels might have been forced to portray some woeful roles in WCW, but at least he didn't have to wrestle with his junk flapping about the place.

DEAF C.M. PUNK

It's no secret that WWE didn't have big plans for C.M. Punk when he signed with the company in 2005. Despite (or, rather, because of) his status as one of the finest talents on the Indie scene, Punk's work during a dark match was torn to shreds by Triple H, Michael Hayes, Arn Anderson. and Shawn Michaels before he was shipped to OVW for further seasoning.

In September 2005, while Punk was training in OVW, it was revealed that WWE's creative department had come up with a gimmick for his debut: Punk was going to be promoted as the first ever deaf wrestler. Yup, that's was the best that WWE creative could come up with for the former Ring of Honour Champion.

There were apparently many *hilarious* backstage segments planned for deaf Punk, in what would have been a sickening and blatant attempt at cheap heat from WWE. Can you imagine how hard it would have been for Punk to kayfabe the gimmick in public? Luckily, wiser heads prevailed, namely Paul Heyman, who vehemently argued against the idea and insisted that Punk be allowed to portray his 'Straight-Edge Superstar' gimmick, which Heyman felt would make him the relaunched ECW's most marketable star.

Ultimately Heyman was proved to be correct. Punk toiled away without office support for years before breaking through and becoming one of WWE's biggest and most-talked about stars, before taking his ball and going home the night after the 2014 *Royal Rumble*, quitting wrestling for a career in the real fighting world of UFC.

THE POSSE UNCHAINED

Early in their careers, future WWE Hall Of Famer Booker and his brother Stevie Ray competed as a tag team known as The Ebony Experience in the Global Wrestling Federation. When that promotion went bust WCW were quick to pounce with offers for the better talent so that they could get there first before the WWF. The Ebony Experience were amongst those hired, and the gimmick first proposed to them was one of the most racist in modern wrestling history.

The original plan was for the brothers to be black slaves won by Colonel Robert Parker during a gambling spree. Booker and Stevie (who would have gone by the names Kane and Kole) were to be led to the thing by Parker with chains around their neck, forced to do heelish deeds under duress. Really they would be babyfaces beneath that, trying to overcome oppression and "break free of their chains."

Picture Harlem Heat in the role of Jamie Foxx's Django from Quentin Tarantino's *Django Unchained*, with Colonel Parker as Leonardo DiCaprio's Calvin Candie. For all intents and purposes, Booker and Stevie would be mandingo fighters, forced to do the bidding of the rich white man against their will.

It was incredibly close to happening. On a *WCW Saturday Night* taping in June 1993, Parker introduced his new team The Posse, which was Harlem Heat in their slave-wear and shackles. Somebody in WCW's hierarchy was paying attention and evidently realised that this wildly racially insensitive gimmick would absolutely not fly under the Turner umbrella, so it never reached television.

TRIPLE H IN THE NWO

In 2002, WWE witnessed the return of the nWo led by the original trio of Hulk Hogan, Kevin Nash and Scott Hall. However, Hogan quickly got over as a babyface, Nash was injured, and Hall got himself fired, leaving the faction in tatters. WWE were determined to utilise the name so reimagined the faction, turning it into the onscreen coming together of the Kliq, led by Shawn Michaels. On the road to *SummerSlam '02*, plans were in place for a match featuring the nWo's Kevin Nash with teammate Shawn Michaels in his corner, against Triple H, who was refusing to join his former Kliq friends in their new faction. This match would have been significant as WWE was planning for Triple H—who always had to have his hand in everything—to then take up Michaels' invitation to join him and the Kliq in the New World Order. Unfortunately, Nash injured himself again prior to *SummerSlam* which proved to be the final nail in the coffin of the nWo's brief WWE existence. Who knows what creative direction the WWE would have taken if the nWo had continued with Nash, Michaels and Triple H. Chances are they would have become the dominant faction in WWE and Evolution would never have happened. Nash and Triple H would end up feuding in 2003 once Nash recovered, culminating in an uninspiring Hell In A Cell Match at *Badd Blood '03*.

CHRISTIAN'S BLUE DOT

It is often said that Vince McMahon likes doing wrestling one way and one way alone; his way. He is unwilling to waiver on his opinion that wrestlers should be big, chiselled-jawed, jacked-up guys who look like they could kick your ass. They certainly shouldn't be short, skinny, or ugly. While McMahon had ceded under intense pressure on rare occasion and allowed the likes of Daniel Bryan and C.M. Punk to slip through the net, others have not been so fortunate. According to former WWE writers Court Bauer and Alex Greenfield, McMahon struggled with his "ugly" face. As Bauer recalls, "One time Vince didn't like a wrestler because of the way he looked. It was Christian. He doesn't like Christian, and wanted to put a blue dot over his face, and he asked the production team if there was a way to put in a blue dot, censoring his face. It never happened because it was just so ridiculous, not to mention expensive." Greenfield confirms that the idea was formed on a flight to the UK around 2005, when McMahon was struggling with Christian's "ratty" face: "We were on the plane one time shortly after I started, and Vince was just like 'I just don't like his face. His face really bothers me.' I was like, 'He's ugly, Vince?' 'No, it's not that he's ugly, it's just, I don't know, it's ratty!'" Vince had found inspiration from a Kennedy rape case in the '90s: "Some heir of the Kennedy fortune I guess got arrested for rape in the 90's at some point. When the woman who was accusing him was on the stand, all of the networks put a blue dot over her face. Vince was like, 'You know what we should do? We should put a blue dot over his face whenever he comes out.'" Production was like, 'Do you know how expensive it would be to put a CG dot on his face? It's not going to happen.'"

'COWBOY' BRET HART

During Vince McMahon's expansion drive in the early 80s his method of attacked tended to be going to local promoters and offering them two options. Either he would buy them out and they could bow out of the business gracefully, or he would come after their towns and talent, leaving them penniless and embarrassed. Most told the cocky upstart where to go, with the exception of Stu Hart. The grizzled veteran promoter of Stampede Wrestling was smart enough to realise that McMahon was soon going to run the entire business, so he sold his declining territory to the WWF chairman for a cool $1,000,000. Purchasing Stampede gave McMahon access to Hart's contacts and venues is Canada, as well as the vast array of talent on his roster.

One of those was twenty-six-year-old Bret Hart, Stu's son, who started working for the WWF in August 1984 alongside fellow Stampede alum The Dynamite Kid. McMahon had no real plans for Hart, who he considered to be undersized in an era of true giants, other than a body on the roster who could wrestle on the undercard at live events. However, fellow Canadian Pat Patterson recognised Hart's potential and wanted to help make him into a WWF Superstar by giving him a gimmick. He suggested playing off Hart's Calgary upbringing – a city famous for its annual Calgary Stampede rodeo show – and turning him into a cowboy. It was proposed that Hart would come to the ring on a live horse while donning a tacky flashing hat and spurs in place of wrestling boots. Hart could not think of anything he would enjoy portraying less. He was a wrestler's wrestler, a no gimmicks, no nonsense performer who took himself seriously and was proud of his in-ring ability. He did not want to be another Vince McMahon cartoon. Plus, he despised country music and cowboys, or anything relating to rodeo.

Hart did not have the political savvy or company tenure to reject the idea out of hand, so he danced around the subject while he considered his options. When his brother-in-law Jim Neidhart came in from Stampede in early 1985, Hart decided to pitch the idea of teaming with him instead, deciding he might quit the WWF if they rejected the idea and forced him to do the hokey cowboy act. Fortunately for Hart, and for pro wrestling lovers everywhere, the WWF saw sense and put Hart with Neidhart to form the Hart Foundation. However, the cowboy gimmick remained on the shelf. In 1993, the WWF were so excited by the prospect that they gave the gimmick to two different acts, tag team The Smoking Gunns and Memphis wrestling standout (and the promoter's son) Jeff Jarrett. The latter was the closest to Patterson's vision for Hart, forced to croon country music songs while decked in a light-up hat and jacket. He even once rode a horse to the ring.

TORI - SABLE'S SISTER

Rather than the obsessive fan with eyes only for Sable gimmick that Tori (Terri Poch) debuted in WWE, the original plan was to have the pair a little closer. Initially, Tori was going to be revealed as Sable's long lost sister—which could have worked given their physical similarities—and the pair would still feuded, presumably because Sable had been a massive bitch to her in their childhoods, or had ignored her since she found fame. Jealous younger sibling often works well, as proven by the classic Owen Hart-Bret Hart feud years earlier. Saying that, sister siblings have been a mixed bag in the industry, so perhaps it's best that they went with the stalker fan angle instead.

'G.I. JOE' SCOTT HALL

Having turned some heads in WCW with his Rick Rude-alike Diamond Studd gimmick, Scott Hall almost joined Paul E Dangerously's Dangerous Alliance, but instead made his way out of the door to the WWF. Having made the promotional jump, Hall was met with a proposition by Vince McMahon. To channel Hall's army brat past, McMahon wanted to portray him as a G.I. Joe-style babyface, taking advantage of his "military knowledge". It sounds incredibly boring, and Hall thought so too. Instead, Hall countered by essentially pitching the movie *Scarface*, which McMahon had never seen. McMahon loved the idea even more that G.I. Hall, and Razor Ramon was born.

THE GOBBLEDY-TAKER

Along with global megastars such as Hulk Hogan and Steve Austin, The Undertaker is perhaps one of the most recognisable characters in the history of modern professional wrestling. At the very least, he is the most enduring. The Dead Man's supernatural shenanigans, his undeniable presence, and a staunch dedication to upholding kayfabe have ensured that his unmatchable aura has remained intact for over twenty-five years. The Undertaker is a franchise in his own right. But would his remarkable legacy have been held in such reverence had he made his debut by... hatching out of a giant egg?

Astonishingly, there were at one point plans in place to do exactly that. When Vince McMahon signed Mark Calaway in late 1990, he concocted an ingenious idea to hype his debut. He would have him hatch out of a giant egg. The egg was taken on tour and could be seen at live events around the country, with WWF television shows promoting the hatching of the egg at *Survivor Series '90* with a mysterious new superstar inside. According to Mick Foley, ""I used to ride with Undertaker years ago and I had heard that he was going to be debuting as The Eggman."

That's right, The Eggman. Now, I realise that on paper the concept of an undead wizard with supernatural healing powers is perhaps even more out there than that of a man hatching from an egg. Nevertheless, the very thought of it now with the benefit of having seen Undertaker's career develop from oddball gimmick into legendary performer makes for a galling mental image. The chances of The Eggman going on a *WrestleMania* winning streak had the gimmick came to pass, are remote at best.

Fortunately for all involved, Vince came to his senses and realised he could not introduce a performer as imposing as Calaway from a giant egg, instead reimagining him after an old Western mortician and dubbing him Kane The Undertaker. Calaway worked a series of bouts under the Kane moniker prior to his onscreen debut at *Survivor Series* as the mystery fourth man on Ted DiBiase's team, though by then the forename had been dropped. That left an unusual situation where after *Survivor Series* WWF television would refer to Undertaker, briefly, as Kane, due to the nature of advanced taping.

As for the giant egg? Well, even Vince McMahon was not sure what to do, so much so that he didn't even tell his right-hand man Pat Patterson what his plan was. "It was a complete surprise to me. Vince wanted to keep it a surprise," says Patterson, "You know who I thought it was gonna be? I thought it was gonna be Ric Flair." It was not Ric Flair. Instead it was Hector Guerrero, brother of the late Eddie Guerrero, donning a giant turkey outfit with enormous golf ball eyes. Fans booed it out of the building, and following a disastrous appearance at Madison Square Garden a few weeks later where a spotlight temporarily blinded Guerrero and caused him to take a prat fall into the ring, the gimmick was shelved.

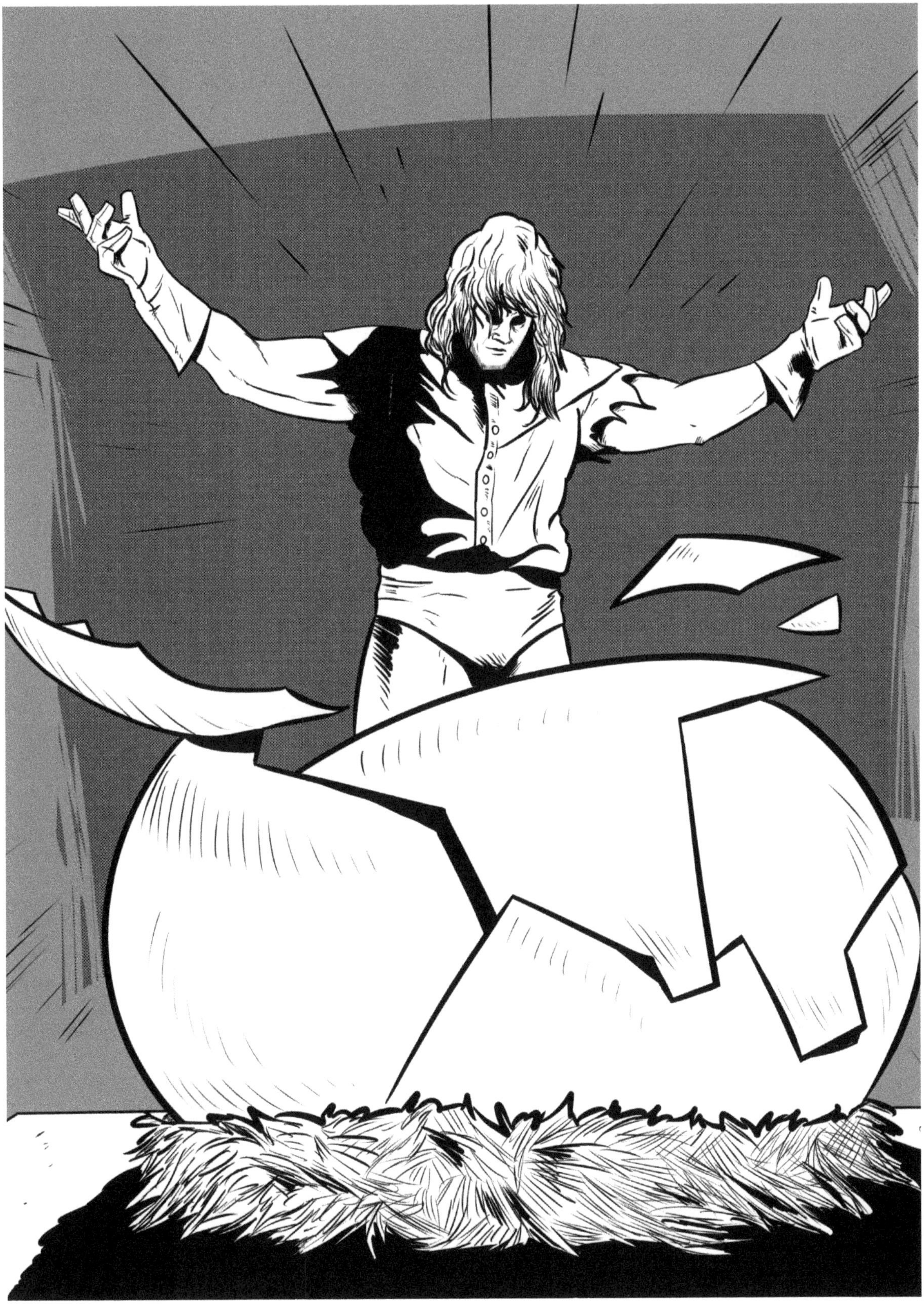

The original idea for the black-clad, riot-gear team known as The Shield, fittingly enough involved shields. Actual real-life shields, made of plastic. As one of the faction's former members Roman Reigns notes, it was not a good look:

"Yeah, we debuted at Survivor Series - the coolest part of that is we were supposed to have like shields. It was really… for lack of a better word… it was really lame. We had like, literal riot shields. Fiberglass riot shields with the word 'SHIELD' written up it.

"We were like … 'everyone will know who we are, jeez.' We just pictured trying to get into the ring with these things. Like, for years now … you go into the ring a certain way, and you're not usually carrying a huge, plastic shield.

"So, we just had this terrifying nightmare of not being able to, like, slide in and we're like stuck. We can't get in and we're looking up and there's Ryback standing over us, and we've completely blown the whole debut.

"So, immediately, Vince was like, 'What, are you guys, wussies? You need that?' We're like, 'No.' And he's like, 'Good, leave them,' and we just ran in there and we beat the dog-piss out of Ryback and put him through the table."

THE SHIELDED SHIELD

PSYCHOPATH SAMOA JOE

By 2009, Samoa Joe had achieved a lot in TNA. Since joining the company in 2005, he had been a focal point of main event storylines—such as his classic series with Kurt Angle—captured the X Division Title on a number of occasions, and became TNA Heavyweight Champion in 2008.

In early-2010, things change in TNA. Hulk Hogan and Eric Bischoff had recently come on board and were shouting from the rooftops about how they—alongside Vince Russo—were going to take the company to the next level. Despite the influx of major names such as Jeff Hardy, Rob Van Dam and, erm, The Nasty Boys, Samoa Joe still seemed set to have a featured spot on the roster.

Not long after the arrival of the former WCW brain-trust, TNA filmed an angle that saw Joe kidnapped by unidentified masked men and removed from television. Typically for TNA, the abduction was never explained. Instead, Joe simply came back a month after disappearing and resumed his duties as though nothing had happened, with TNA announcers specifically told not to mention it.

There was a plan in place though. The original angle called for Joe to be reinvented as a psychopathic character, portrayed as a man who had completely lost his mind. The fact nothing came of such a heavily-hyped angle only hurt TNA, and did little for Joe either. He'd later fall out with Vince Russo backstage, which led to a demotion on screen.

It is difficult to say if the psychopath shtick would have led to anything substantial or a return to TNA main events, it would have all depended on how quickly scatterbrain Russo got fed up of the gimmick. With the correct push and sensible, believable storytelling, it would have likely helped get Joe over as the future of TNA. Instead he lost interest in wrestling and started to phone in his performances, never able to recapture the magic that had made him a star between 2005-2010.

HEEL JOHN CENA

After rapping his way into the hearts and minds of WWE fans, John Cena wanted to throw his position as top babyface out of the window for a while in 2006. The leader of Cenation lobbied hard for Edge to defeat him at *Unforgiven '06* which as per pre-match stips would have sent him to *SmackDown*. After taking a break he would return as a heel, reigniting his feud with Kurt Angle only this time with the roles reversed. However, his feud with Edge got over so well that Cena became a bona fide megastar as a result. The disappointment he showed after beating Edge at *Unforgiven* gave away how he really felt about the lost possibility of a heel turn.

LOUIE 'CHRIS FARLEY' SPICOLLI

Having battled drug addiction throughout his career, Louie Spicolli came to WCW looking for a new opportunity and a fresh start. He found it in an "nWo pledge" role that saw him cast as a hanger-on to Scott Hall, charged with proving his worth by harassing the likes of Larry Zbyszko. Impressed with what he was seeing, Eric Bischoff put Spicolli on commentary, where he immediately flourished. That led to Bischoff pitching the idea of Spicolli becoming WCW's Chris Farley, playing up the goofy and comedic side of his character. Tragically Spicolli died of an overdose in a hauntingly similar manner to Farley before the idea could play out.

DEAF, MUTE EDGE

According to Adam 'Edge' Copeland, there was a pretty bold idea for the direction of his gimmick in the early days. Prior to the debut of his Edge character in 1998, Vince Russo had pitched making Copeland a deaf mute. The idea was due to Russo's lack of faith in the wrestler's mic skills, as well as his annoyance with Copeland's lack of enthusiasm towards other ideas he had suggested. Those include Copeland becoming a Jim Morrison-type poetry reading character, and teaming with Sean Morley to form the New Midnight Express (Adorable Adam and Sensual Sean). Thankfully they settled on "moody goth" and Edge was born.

COMEDY RUSEV

WWE weren't entirely certain what to do with Rusev when he first came into the company. In fact, when clips of him in NXT were shown to the creative team, they burst out laughing thanks to the unintentionally hilarious 1970s feel of his character. That almost inspired a creative direction that would see Rusev used as a comedy character:

"We started coming up with pitches for him as a comedy act, but we were told that Triple H envisioned Rusev as a monster heel so we had better forget about the character being played for laughs," explains former WWE writer Kevin Eck.

That proved to be a wise move, as did the decision to avoid Vince McMahon's questions about whether Lana should remain part of the gimmick, which Eck says probably have been fatal: "I didn't think Rusev had a great chance of being a success even with Lana by his side, but without her he had zero chance."

'SILVERBACK' MARK HENRY

Unfortunately, it seems WWE is never far away from pitching politically incorrect gimmicks. One example came in 2007 when Vince McMahon suggested rebranding Mark Henry as Silverback—a potentially racist moniker loaded with offensive overtones. For those unaware, a Silverback is a giant gorilla, the leader of the pack. McMahon likely only thought of the gimmick because Henry was built like a gorilla, missing the obvious "monkey" connotations. Henry didn't miss them: "A lot of people remember the Silverback thing. Honestly, I could not do it. I told them, 'I can't do that. I got two little black kids at home.'" Vince just never learns.

RIC FLAIR IS SPARTACUS

Given that the man was still talked about now in glowing terms decades later, it seems impossible to imagine that people thought Ric Flair was old hat in the early-90's. However, that's exactly what then-boss of WCW, Jim Herd thought about the 'Nature Boy'. In his infinite wisdom, he came up with a concept that could help rectify the situation and make Flair relevant again. Instead of coming to the ring adorned in his trademark robes, Herd wanted Flair to cut his hair, trade his Armani suits for suits of armour, and become a Gladiator called Spartacus.

It makes for completely ludicrous reading now, because Flair would go on to wrestle full-time for another seventeen years or so following that, including two successful spells in the WWF/WWE where he was absolutely relevant, and he did not have to saddle himself with a ridiculous gimmick to remain so. Incredibly, the pro wrestling legend did actually consider going through with it enough that he cut off most of his bleach-blonde locks, but that was as far as he was willing to go. Instead he quit the company and signed with the World Wrestling Federation.

Herd's plan would have alienated much of the fan base, who still went wild for Flair. To put things into perspective, a WWE equivalent would be if Vince McMahon suddenly decided The Undertaker should dye his hair blonde and pretend to be a marine. It's not hard to picture the negative response from fans if such a thing were to happen. That was the kind of thing facing Flair and WCW in the early-90's, and it's undoubtedly a good thing that the idea never went any further.

THE HUNCHBACKS

Jim Herd cultivated something of a reputation when he attempted to repackage WCW by adding in increasingly zany gimmicks to appeal to younger audiences. As well as coming up with hare-brained characters such as the Ding Dongs, he also formulated a plan to introduce a duo called the Hunchbacks, who would have been played by the legendary jobber tandem the Mulkey brothers. Herd was confident this was the greatest idea for a tag team ever: "They got the big hump on their back, you know, and ya' can't pin 'em. They are an unbeatable tag team and that's how we'll sell 'em." Booker Ole Anderson quickly disproved Herd's crackpot theory: "All right, Jim, you book the Hunchbacks, build them up, they're undefeated. Then you book them with me and Arn. As soon as I tag in, I'm going to take one of them down, I'm going to slap an arm bar on him and I'm going to make him submit. He is going to give up. I just beat your unbeatable team." Suffice to say, all plans for the Hunchbacks were dropped.

MIGHTY MOUSE

At one stage prior to former Indie standout Adrian Neville receiving the call up to join the main WWE roster, discussions were doing the rounds that Vince McMahon wanted to saddle him with a Mighty Mouse gimmick. It was a role he had long been determined to do, having considered something similar for Chris Candido back in the 90s. Thankfully, the Mighty Mouse tie-in was merely inspiration, there were no plans—or at least not serious ones—to dress Neville as a mouse. Neville played down the rumours as fan scuttlebutt, then a few weeks later turned up wearing a cape (which he had never done in NXT) and playing a superhero-style character.

MUHAMMAD HASSAN - WORLD CHAMPION

The anti-West gimmick of the Arab-American Muhammad Hassan gained significant momentum in early 2005, not to mention notoriety. To many it seemed as if Hassan was on track to follow in the footsteps of workers with similar "evil foreigner" gimmicks such as The Iron Sheik and Bret Hart (who was an anti-American heel in 1997) and become WWE Champion. And indeed, Hassan was such a strong heel that WWE's creative team were planning for him to win the World Heavyweight Championship in the summer of 2005, in the process breaking the record set by Randy Orton one year earlier and becoming the youngest ever World Champion in WWE history. However, the tragic terrorist attacks in London on the 7/7 2005 meant that those plans had to be shelved. Rather than Hassan going on to defeat Batista for the title at *SummerSlam* as per the original plan, the title incumbent defeated JBL in a throwaway match. WWE were soon forced to drop the Hassan character altogether due to the negative press he was receiving. While unfortunate, they were left with no choice.

MARIA MONTANA

After being released by WWE in 2010, ex-Diva Maria Kanellis revealed that she had pitched a number of angles to get her over as a top woman in the division. However, the ideas she pitched would be considered by most to be absurd. In her big pitch, Maria suggested that she would play two different characters simultaneously. Well, it did work for Hannah Montana. One side of the character coin would see Maria playing her usual innocent ditzy blonde babyface character, while the other would be much a darker heel version. The evil doppelgänger was planned to be a dark-haired (a sure fire sign of evil), aggressive rock chick with a bad attitude. She wanted both characters to be dating the same, oblivious wrestler, which would all lead to a title shot that would see the personas merging into one Super Maria when she smashed a mirror. Unsurprisingly, creative rebuked her suggestions, just as they did another idea she had to blackmail Dolph Ziggler over a sex tape she'd secretly filmed with him. Why Dolph would need blackmailing to keep that under wraps is a mystery.

THE ULTIMATE VADER

In 1987, Antonio Inoki came up with a gimmick that he wanted to use in New Japan Pro Wrestling to create a new foreign star: Big Van Vader. The name was inspired by Japanese folklore - Vader loosely translated means 'Emperor's warrior' – and the gimmick called for whomever portrayed the role to don a metal helmet based on Samurai armour.

Inoki wanted someone imposing to play the role and he had a number of candidates in mind. Amongst them were Continental Championship Wrestling monster Lord Humongous (Sidney 'Sycho Sid' Eudy) and AWA's Bull Power (Leon White), but his first choice was a muscle-bound ex-bodybuilder from WCCW called The Dingo Warrior (the future Ultimate Warrior).

However, Inoki had seen very little of Warrior in the ring and changed his mind after seeing more of his work. Despite his impressive physique and boundless energy, he felt he was not good enough between the ropes to compete with his world-class roster. Instead, Inoki went with his second choice, Leon White.

White was allowed to make an immediate impact by delivering a crushing beating to Inoki, who had already wrestled a long match against Riki Choshu. The beating Vader gave to Inoki was so severe that the audience in Sumo Hall rioted, causing New Japan to get banned from the venue for over a year. Two years after his debut in New Japan, Vader was pushed to the pinnacle of the company when he defeated legendary grappler Shinya Hashimoto to win the vacant IWGP Heavyweight Championship. White made the gimmick his own and became synonymous with the Vader character, playing it on the international stage with global powerhouses WCW and the WWF.

It did not turn out too badly for the jilted Dingo Warrior either. A few months after Inoki did his about-turn, Warrior was offered a contract with the WWF. Rebranded as the Ultimate Warrior, he went on to become WWF Champion and one of the biggest stars in all of wrestling. As Warrior once put it in his own interminable manner, "Vader didn't become as popular as Ultimate Warrior!"

Curiously, and somewhat fittingly, Warrior's final ever match in the WWF was a pinfall victory over Vader on June 25, 1996, bringing the pair's history full circle.

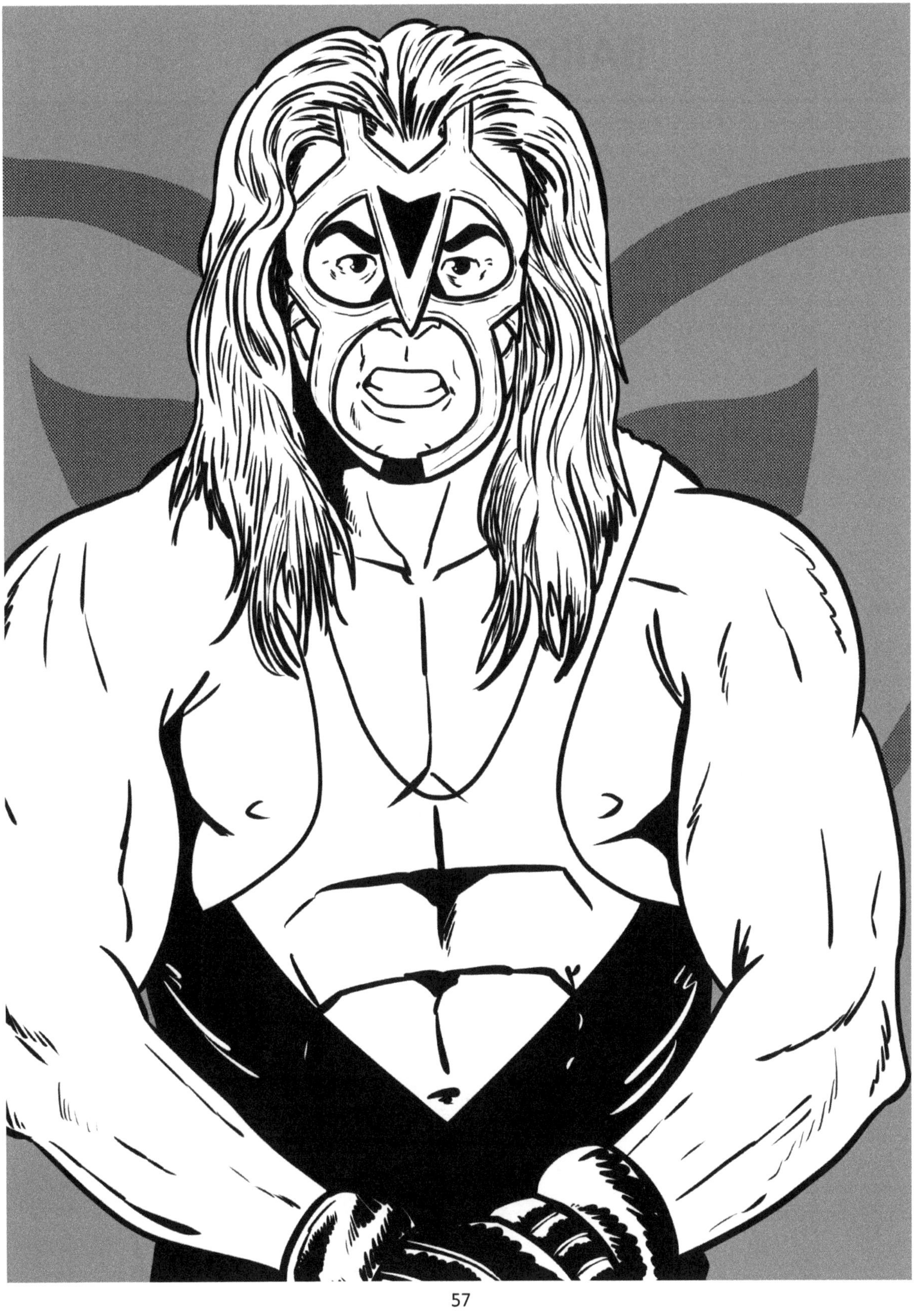

BARON VON BAVA

In the pantheon of dreadful gimmick pitches, few are as awful as a character that former WWE writer Dan Madigan pitched for the totally clueless Jon Heidenreich. It was a gimmick in such poor taste that not only did it make it nowhere near TV, but it also forced Vince McMahon to leave the room in disgust after hearing it.

Madigan's idea was for Heidenreich to come in as Baron von Bava, a cryogenically frozen Nazi Stormtrooper from the 1940s who had been frozen in ice, only to be thawed out by Paul Heyman some sixty years later. He would be intent on carrying out the work of Adolf Hitler and would goose-step to the ring.

It sounds almost fantastical, but this is a pitch that genuinely happened. Not only is the idea extremely distasteful and totally out there, but having Paul Heyman (who is Jewish) manage a Nazi cyborg? Come on! In order to fully illustrate his idea, Madigan apparently began goose-stepping around the writer's room himself as his colleagues sat in stunned silence.

On the whole debacle, Madigan said to *Power Slam* magazine in 2008, "I thought these were good ideas: inside my mind, it worked out well." In reality it did not. Madigan was let go by the company not long after and all talk of Baron von Bava ceased to exist.

Another writer from the same period suggested it was a nail in the coffin of Madigan's WWE career: "From that day forward, Dan was a marked man, his ideas were cast aside and not even judged."

ALBERT STEELE

Matt Bloom has a lot to thank George Steele for. It was Steele who first introduced Bloom to WWF developmental trainer Dr. Tom Prichard, who was impressed with the younger's size and intelligence, so signed him to a deal. Bloom very nearly had his career forever associated with the green-tongued 'Animal' not long after that. When WWF creative bods first saw the gigantic hairy bear now known as Baldo plying his trade in Memphis developmental league Power Pro Wrestling, they immediately began formulating ideas for his main roster debut. Baldo was viewed as a can't-miss prospect due to his size and unique look, and they were determined to give him a memorable gimmick.

As with most WWF creations the idea they came up with was down to the accentuation of one of Bloom's most interesting features: his incredibly hairy torso. One of the team commented, "Y'know, he kinda reminds me of George Steele with that big hairy back." With that the kernel of an idea was formed, and it was soon suggested that Bloom should be promoted as George Steele's son, complete with his own green tongue and a penchant for dining on turnbuckle pads. They could even have Steele manage him.

Vince McMahon ultimately decided against it. 1998-99 was a time where the WWF was trying to retcon its past and only look to the future, so an homage gimmick was not going to cut it in the Attitude Era. Instead Bloom became the pierced giant Albert, the storyline tattooist for the equally odd-looking Droz.

FEATURE:

BY VINCE RUSSO

10 INSIGHTS INTO WORKING WITH VINCE MCMAHON

Before I begin this piece, let me first clarify that this is indeed designed to be a "tribute" to my former boss, Vincent Kennedy McMahon. Now, even if he catches wind of this, by being "smartened up" by some stooge in his office, and he views my insights in a different light, then that will simply just be his ego talking.

You see, Vince McMahon was one of the most unique and eccentric human beings that I've ever had the pleasure to both know and work with. The truth is, even though he's responsible for a roster of over a hundred "characters", let the truth now be known, that HE perhaps is the greatest "gimmick" of them all!

Everything I'm about to share with you - sides of the boss that many have NEVER seen before - are the qualities and uniqueness that simply make Vince, Vince. And, to put it as honestly as I can - I wouldn't want him any other way!

Vince Creates An Atmosphere Of Mistrust

Even though it was done with non-malice, Vince just loved stirring the sh*t up with those in his inner circle. He did it for years between me and Bruce Prichard, and especially me and JR. You know the game: say something to me, then say something to them, back to me, yada-yada-yada.

Now, let me make this perfectly clear to you: even though there was no ill intent, and Vince was doing it for his own sense of entertainment, it did indeed drive wedges between all of us. No serious gaps, mind you, but enough to just give you a sense of "mistrust".

Vince was just great at playing that game. I don't know, maybe he just felt like a little competition would fuel our fires.

Vince Had Zero Social Life!

This is an absolute shoot. In the five years that I worked at the WWE, I always arrived at work before the bell, and left way after its final ding-dong. I took great pride in working for one of the greatest companies in the world, let's face it: it was my childhood dream. However, regardless of my aggressive work ethic, no matter how early I arrived, or how late I left - Vince's car was there. This is no joke. If I got in at 7am - his car was already there. If I left at 10pm - his car was STILL there!!! In other words - the guy just never left the office.

I'm sure that many of those early hours and late nights he spent at Titan Tower could have been attributed to his obsession of pumping iron. Vince had a beautiful gym built in the lower level of the office and he spent many hours there. He was never home, he was always there, in the office or in the gym.

Now, hand-in-hand with this possessiveness leads to another "somewhat" known fact. Vince has NO social life whatsoever. NONE. ZERO. NADA. I know when I worked for him from 94-99, he had very few "real" friends.

Now, I'm not talking about the boys, or Patterson, I'm talking about REAL FRIENDS outside of the business. He just never "hung" with anybody to the extent of what I was an eyewitness to. It was always all work, and no play, even though to him - the work WAS his play.

I can even remember one time so vividly, where he actually told me that he brought Linda to see a movie - Krippendorf's Tribe, staring Richard Dreyfuss. I'll never forget the name of that picture because I remember saying to myself, "You never leave work, you probably never take out your wife, and when you finally do you go see KRIPPENDORF'S FREAKIN' TRIBE?!!!

So here's where I have to point something out: this almost in-human obsession and commitment to his company, is what makes the WWE the juggernaut that it is today. nobody and I mean NOBODY will ever come along and outwork the boss.

NOBODY.

And for that level of dedication, you have to just respect the guy.

The King Of Sports Entertainment Knows Nothing About Sports

All right, here's the thing: if you're a "GUY", then you have to be talking sports each and every day of your life. Now, add to that: if you are a "GUY" who hangs around athletes every day, you HAVE TO BE talking about sports ALL THE TIME! Right?

Wrong.

In all the hours that I spent with Vince, I never heard him talk about sports once. Not once.

Football, baseball, basketball, women's field hockey... Nothing. Never. I remember a specific time in 1997, when my beloved San Francisco Giants were in the playoffs and they were facing off against the Florida Marlins. Man, I was so jacked for this series, but I can remember quite vividly, that one of the games aired while I was working at Vince's house.

Now, this is how loyal a die-hard Giants fan I am - I didn't care. I was going to ask Vince if I could leave school early today, so I could go home and watch the baseball game!!!

I remember that in approaching Vince I was real nervous, not because of what I was asking him, but because I wasn't sure whether or not he would be able to relate to my love for the game. If he didn't understand, then it was more important to him that I stay there and finish up.

The outcome: Vince let me leave, and the freaking' Giants lost!

The Hideous Looking Office

OK, so, I've been a fan of the WWE since probably around say 1972 and in 1993-1994 I get a job with the company. That's a span of 22 years. So, put yourself in my shoes... Can you even imagine what was going through my head as I prepared myself for my first official meeting with Vincent Kennedy McMahon?

Now, I had actually met Vince about a year earlier... and let me stop to talk about that for a moment.

It was probably around early 1992, when I was working on a radio show on Long Island. At the time the steroid issue was HOT and HEAVY concerning use and abuse by WWF wrestlers. Of course, the guy in the hot seat was Vince McMahon.

In an effort to be active opposed to re-active, Vince conducted a press conference in NYC, where he laid out the new steroid testing policy that the Federation was putting in place, as an effort to squash the problem. It was there where I first met Vince.

I have worked with and met many superstars both inside of wrestling - and outside it - but to this very day, I had never been around one man with such power and energy you could feel it in a room the moment he walked in. Vince just had this aura surrounding him that told you that the man was something very special.

Okay, back to hideous office.

So, I psyche myself up for my first one-on-one encounter with Vince; this time on an employer/employee level. YES, I'm nervous as hell, wouldn't you be?!

I wait in the "outer-office" of Vince's "inner-office", which seems likes days. WEEKS even. Finally, I get the call in. OK, this is what I see - to paint the picture as clearly as I possibly can - it looked like A ZEBRA GOT INTO A FIGHT WITH HIS PENCIL SHARPNER.

There was this red velour carpet on the floor, and zebra print on the walls. I swear, I had never seen anything like it before.

The good news was that I was so taken back by the interior design that the nervousness I had entering this - I don't know what - completely disappeared!

"There Is No Sick"

"There is no sick". That was a direct quote from Vince McMahon to me, while I tried to work through a pay-per-view and TV taping when in actuality I should have been in a hospital. Yes, I was that sick.

I don't remember the year, or the event, all I remember is Ken Shamrock and The Rock had a match. I was so sick backstage that I was actually soaking wet with sweat, as I watched the show wearing a heavy over coat while SHAKING. I just wanted to go home, that's it. But, when you work for Vince, you go to work, there is no other option.

That infamous line came from Vince the night prior at our production meeting when I was on the verge of DEATH while sitting next to him. After about an hour into the meeting, Vince looked at me somewhat annoyed and said, "What's wrong with you?" "Vince, I'm Sick", I said. He looked me dead in the eye and delivered the line, "THERE IS NO SICK."

I never forget that to this day.

And trust me, he wasn't kidding. This is a guy who gets IRATE when he sneezes. IRATE! You know why? Because he couldn't CONTROL the sneeze. He also never - NEVER - wears a coat in the winter regardless of how cold it is. The frightening thing was that his son, Shane, was slowly, but surely, taking on all his father's "quirks".

Wrestling Always Comes First

One thing that many of you do indeed already know - and I'm just going to confirm - all that matters to Vincent Kennedy McMahon is PROFESSIONAL WRESTLING. That's it. He lives it 24 hours a day, 7 days a week, and has since his father the great Vince McMahon Sr. introduced him to the world when he was just 12 years old.

From those early days, Vince just wanted to follow in his father's footsteps, who by the way - he had just met. At that point in his young life a decision was made that this was going to be his one and only passion in life, and the very thing that he lived for!

Vince's Love For The Garden

Vince held Madison Square Garden to his highest regard. The Mecca of professional sports in New York City was extremely near and dear to his heart. I think MSG represented many things to Vince.

First of all, I'm sure it symbolised to him that he had made IT. A kid growing up in North Carolina, Vince had a tough childhood. His father left home when he was just a baby, bringing his oldest son with him. From there Vince survived abuse to both himself and his mom, through a variety of unruly stepfathers. Fortunately for Vince, he reunited with Vince Sr. at 12 years-old, and the rest is history!

Vince McMahon Sr. is a member of the Madison Square Garden Hall of Fame, and this is indeed the fact as to why this building means so much to him. I can remember on my first visit to the Garden as an employee of the WWE, I received an earful from Vince because I didn't wear a jacket and tie to the event.

Vince himself pulled me aside, and explained to me that his father was enshrined in the Hall of Fame there, and what that meant to him. I remember being very touched by that, and having even a greater respect for Vince due to that incident.

Daddy's Little Girl

Vince makes no qualms about it: Stephanie always has been, is, and always will be "Daddy's Little Girl". Whatever picture is painted of Vince by all of us who know him, there is one thing that we will all agree on: he loves his daughter to the ends of the world. Aside for WHO he is, their father/daughter relationship is very traditional.

I think part of the reason that I never went back to the WWE in 2002, was because of the spot that Vince had put Stephanie in once I upped and left the company. Basically, he put her in my spot. With her steering the creative ship, ratings started to falter a bit, and I never held Stephanie responsible for that.

I always felt like those around her who she was depending on at the time were flat out just not delivering.

So here I come to save the day, only issue is that Stephanie would now be my boss. How was that going to work for all parties involved? The answer is simple: at the time it wasn't, so at the end of the day Vince stood by his daughter to protect her perception, and once again I gained even a greater respect for him.

Generosity

Vince was always generous with me from the start. Two things really stand out in my mind that depicts how he rewards his employees when they are delivering for him. Once, my wife, Amy, and I were just looking to get away for a few days.

Catching wind of this, Vince gave us full access to his home in Boca Raton at the time. Amy and I had a blast, we felt like we were in paradise! Vince even had an elevator in that house, the extravagance blew me away!

Another incident that I will never forget came at the boom of the "Attitude Era". I was riding in an elevator with Vince at Titan Tower from his office on the fourth floor, down to the lobby. During that short ride, Vince reached into his coat jacket and took out an envelope and handed it to me. "Here, Vince, this is for you."

Vince exited the elevator and went on his way. I went back up to my office on the second floor, closed the door, and opened the envelope which he handed me. It was a check with many, many zeroes. More money than I had ever seen at once in my entire life.

Deep Down, He's Just A Regular Guy

Deep down he was a regular guy, that was who Vince McMahon was to me.

Look, as time went on, Vince and I would have our differences and go our separate ways - that stuff just happens. And even at the end when he made a comment about my family that I just couldn't forgive him for, it never changed my view of him. You see, when you can get through the parody, and the facade, and the Vince McMahon that is perceived, and he no doubt helped create, you find a guy who I just think wants to be "one of the guys".

The Vince I remember is the guy sitting at his dining room table where we wrote TV, hair dishevelled, and sweat pants. If you want me to get really raw here... there was even some man-gas spread on those special occasions!

That's the guy I'll remember, and that's the guy that I'll always love.

BOOKING

PLANS CAN CHANGE AT THE DROP OF A HAT...

VADER - WWF CHAMPION

Vader – after Vince McMahon was convinced by Jim Ross and Jim Cornette – was pencilled in to defeat Shawn Michaels at SummerSlam '96. McMahon was not yet sold on Vader, who he felt was in poor shape and had displayed attitude problems in a house show series with The Ultimate Warrior.

Nevertheless, Vince agreed to the storyline, which was supposed to culminate at Royal Rumble '97 in Michaels' hometown of San Antonio, where the returning babyface hero would finally conquer his mammoth foe. It was the same overwhelmed underdog booking that the WWF had mastered over the years, and McMahon was convinced it would work for Michaels and finally get him over with a male audience who were rejecting him.

He booked Vader against Michaels around the house show loop so they could get familiar working together, but it only caused problems. Vader was used to working stiff and getting away with it, which elsewhere would have been fine. In the WWF with a much tougher schedule, wrestlers were far less inclined to allow their bodies to take such a beating. During one match, Vader stiffed Michaels so hard that the grumpy Heartbreak Kid warned that if he hit him again, he would have him fired.

Michaels did not have him fired, but he did have the main event program changed. Concerned about the prospect of working with Vader for the next six months, Michaels nixed the program and suggested Sycho Sid step into the role of resident monster instead. The way Michaels saw it, Sid was a clumsy lunk, but at least he worked light. Ultimately, Vader never did win the WWF Championship, though his replacement Sid would have two runs with the belt, one of which afforded him a place in the headline spot at WrestleMania 13.

JOHN CENA CLEANS UP THE STREETS

According to former WWE creative Court Bauer, at some point during John Cena's reign as WWE's unblemished white knight in shining armour, there was a plan to play up his hero status even further. Bauer revealed the craziest pitch he had ever witnessed during his time in WWE was when a writer pitched a drug dealing cartel stable to feud with Cena. Cena would have played the Superman figure, busting guys who made bad decisions and taking out drug lords while preaching clean living to the kids. Unsurprisingly, it didn't make it past the idea stages. Drugs have been an issue for WWE for years, calling attention to it was far too risky.

INTERGALACTIC WARFARE

When ECW debuted on SyFy there were plans to tie-in with the network by presenting an oddball intergalactic angle on the first show that has to be chalked down as one of the strangest ideas WWE have ever had. According to former writer Court Bauer, the plan was to have a wrestler brutally lay the smackdown on a little green man. An alien! Or at least a fellow wrestler dressed as a Martian. Eventually, the gimmick was dropped, and instead the inaugural episode saw the infamous zombie debut instead, presumably because beating up aliens on a network where they were the bread and butter might be considered biting the hand that feeds you.

THE TUBBY VAMPIRE

Who knew that vampirism could be bad for your waist-line? Apparently, that was the reason a planned ECW angle in 2006 featuring a vampire stable led by Attitude Era star Gangrel was scrapped. The pitch was to have the Vampire Warrior team up with Kevin Thorn and Ariel—the tarot-reading fortune teller—as part of a neck-biting faction. Sadly for fans of night walkers, Gangrel's ongoing weight issues delayed the introduction of the stable before it was scrapped altogether when he failed to get in shape. Thorn and Ariel were left to work together, while Gangrel returned to the Indies while also trying his hand at directing pornography.

SYLVAIN GRENIER - MAIN EVENT SUPERSTAR

Sylvain Grenier's inability to make a *Tough Enough* audition due to visa issues might well have been a major blessing in disguise. Thanks to that missed opportunity, Grenier had to enter WWE via a different avenue, joining developmental territory OVW before stepping up to the main roster as part of French anti-American tag team La Résistance. Despite numerous shortcomings that would ultimately cost him his job, Vince McMahon had him pegged to be a star. According to ex-WWE writer Alex Greenfield, McMahon was adamant that the creative team did everything they could to get Grenier over, and even once demanded to know why he was not being better utilised. "Shit like this happened all the time," says Greenfield, "It was inexplicable to me and everyone else where the money was in this guy, or what Vince saw in him. Look, Sylvain was a good-looking guy with decent size, he fit the prototype of the kind of guy Vince likes to become a star, but Sylvain was just freaking terrible and everyone but Vince seemed to know it."

THE RETURN OF THE FOUR HORSEMEN

By former WWE writer George Rutherford:

I was hired to be a creative writer for WWE in April of 2007. The roster at the time boasted some pretty big names, but creatively the company seemed to be in a bit of a drought. Being the new guy on the scene, I desperately hoped to come up with something that would give a shot in the arm to the storylines.

At the time, WWE was about to release the Ric Flair and the Four Horsemen DVD set. I grew up being a huge fan of the Horsemen. They were the first real power stable in wrestling. There would be no DX or NWO without them.

At the time, Ric Flair was (amazingly) still on the active roster and wrestling every week. Former Horseman Chris Benoit, Arn Anderson, Tully Blanchard, Dean Malenko and Barry Windham were all either on the payroll or on "Legend" contracts.

I first pitched the idea to Flair: The Four Horsemen return as a high-powered management team who take over the SmackDown brand. Instead of being the most dominant stable in the ring, they create it.

By offering lucrative incentives to talent, they would pull wrestlers away from the influence of Vince McMahon and unite them under the banner of the Horsemen. It would have been a nice promotional tool for the DVD and a fun way to build interest in SmackDown.

Flair loved it. He was all for it. When the idea was pitched to the powers that be, it was met with a pretty lukewarm reception. It was essentially relegated to the "perhaps if Hell freezes over" file.

Flair, still clearly believing in the popularity of the Horsemen, pulled a subtle, but awesome move one night after RAW went off the air. He had just finished the main event match of the night. The monitors had faded to black.

As he slowly walked up the ramp to go backstage, he stopped, turned to the audience, and lifted his hand into the air with four fingers up (the sign of the Four Horsemen). The crowed went absolutely berserk. Regrettably, I never got the chance to talk with Ric about it afterward.

With that one gesture though, I felt the idea was completely validated.

TYSON AND HOGAN! TYSON AND HOGAN!

When fans and historians alike discuss the one pivotal moment that turned things around for the WWF during the Monday Night Wars, it is generally accepted that the Montreal Screwjob was inadvertently responsible for changing the entire course of the company. If pushed to pick a single segment that was the most important in reshaping the company's fortunes, most would like choose the legendary pull-apart between heat-magnet boxer Mike Tyson and Steve Austin on the January 19, 1998 episode of Monday Night Raw. But what if was not Austin and Tyson at all? What if it was Tyson and Hulk Hogan?

In 1990 Tyson was undefeated in boxing and on top of the world when he stepped into the ring to fight Buster Douglas. While in great shape physically, Tyson had arrogantly taken a laissez-faire attitude to preparing for the fight and thus was not mentally prepared. Douglas on the other hand, fought the fight of his life in memory of his recently deceased mother, and knocked out the previously-invincible Tyson following a flurry in the tenth round. The result sent shockwaves throughout the boxing world, and to this day it is considered one of the all-time biggest upsets in the history of any sport.

The result had a significant impact on the WWF too, because they had booked and promoted Tyson refereeing a blow-off match between Randy Savage and Hulk Hogan on NBC special *The Main Event III* twelve days after the fight. As if often the case when a major star loses in such a shocking manner, Tyson pulled himself from all scheduled appearances (the same thing happened with the similarly unbeatable Ronda Rousey when she was defeated by Holly Holm at *UFC 193* in 2015).

With 'Iron Mike' now unavailable, the WWF hurriedly put together an alternative deal to bring in Buster Douglas for the same role in order to capitalise on his fleeting fame. Douglas did well as Tyson's stand-in, but he did not possess anywhere near the same level of charisma and star power as Tyson would have brought to the table.

Tyson went into a tailspin following the defeat, with the troubled boxer arrested in 1992 on conviction of rape and eventually imprisoned for three years. After his return to boxing he caused further controversy by biting a chunk out of opponent Evander Holyfield's ear, causing him to be banned from boxing. This allowed the WWF to make their move and bring Tyson in to help catapult Steve Austin into the stratosphere. Had he already appeared for the company in 1990, his presence might not have meant quite so much.

THE BALLAD OF TRIPLE H AND STEPHANIE

When Vince Russo abruptly jumped to WCW in late 1999 he left the WWF in the difficult situation of having to come up with resolutions to various angles he had started. One of the most notable was the Stephanie McMahon/Test marriage angle, which would eventually be hastily rewritten with Triple H swooping in for the ending we all saw.

Originally though, Russo says his plan was to have Test turn heel, jilt Stephanie at the altar, and join D-Generation X. A fairly radical departure from the eventual ending.

A year later, another Stephanie love triangle was supposed to end with her running off with Kurt Angle and the pair turning heel as Hunter turned babyface. That betrayal too was nixed.

For a hat-trick of gimmicks that prove the Levesques are not afraid of blurring the reality of their marriage, in 2002 the Chris Jericho/Triple H *WrestleMania* feud was originally intended to focus on Stephanie and Y2J having an affair.

In that case, Triple H said no and turned Jericho into an instrument in his and Steph's divorce feud, robbing the programme of an additional element that may have helped wake the *WrestleMania* crowd who had been wiped out by The Rock and Hulk Hogan's dust up two matches prior.

"I STILL REMEMBER"

By rights, Booker T should have already been World Heavyweight Champion by November 2003. The year started out so promisingly, with da Bookman pushed to the top and challenging Triple H for the belt at WrestleMania XIX. One insultingly racist storyline and high-profile job later, and Booker was on his way back down the card where "his people" (The Game's words) belonged.

Booker spent the next several months either injured or wrestling nothing matches against other no-hopers in the midcard. Then, on the November 10, 2003 Raw, some intrigue: during a backstage segment with Jon Heidenreich, the five-time WCW Champion received a note which stated, "I STILL REMEMBER."

The former G.I. Bro acted with a mixture of confusion and annoyance at the delivery, although he may have just been surprised that WWE were actually given him a storyline. So where did this "I still remember" business lead to? Absolutely nowhere. It was a one-off thing that WWE had already lost interest in by the time Tuesday morning rolled round. Booker went back to having absolutely no direction, and all was right in WWE.

When first pitched, the note was supposed to be the start of a feud between Booker and his former tag team partner Goldust, however, WWE announced a few days later that they would not be renewing Goldust's contract and he was gone by December, ending the feud before it even started. Don't worry, Book: we still remember.

JTG AND "SELF"

Prior to his release in 2010, former Cryme Time member JTG pitched a gimmick for himself involving a Muppet based on himself, which Vince McMahon greenlighted.

"It was my idea, the idea stemmed from this character I used to do in promo class.... [Vince] would give us an exercise where he would say, 'Say anything and you have to cut a promo on it.'

"I can't remember what word he gave me, but there was a few times where I started talking to myself and it was highly entertaining, and I created a new character with a double personality. His name was Self."

Self would have been a Muppet based on JTG's appearance, and would have been "invisible" to anyone backstage. Like a Jiminy Cricket sort of figure.

"The Muppet was going to be my alter ego. It was going to be my conscience, that only the WWE Universe could see. For example, if we're doing a backstage segment and the camera was on it, Self could be right there insulting you, but you wouldn't acknowledge him, you wouldn't see him. Only myself and the WWE Universe would get a big chuckle out of it. So you'd have to be a great actor, because if he's funny, you cannot laugh. I was thinking about getting a comedian to do the voice. Somebody with comedic timing. Or even probably, we could put Hornswoggle in a Muppet suit."

JTG even spoke with creative about bringing Self to the ring, but ultimately it fell apart and he was released shortly afterwards. A shame, because it actually sounds like an idea that had a shot at getting over.

The formation of the New World Order at Bash At The Beach '96 remains one of the most seminal moments in modern wrestling history, in large part due to the shocking nature of long-time babyface and pop culture icon Hulk Hogan turning heel. But it was nearly very different.

When Hogan was first approached by Eric Bischoff with the idea of abandoning Hulkamania and donning the proverbial black hat, Hogan balked at the prospect. He told Bischoff, "Brother, until you have walked a mile in my red and yellow boots, you have no idea." Bischoff vowed to never bring up the subject again, so he was surprised when he received a call from Hogan a few months later asking for a meeting to discuss turning heel. Hogan had seen the waves generated by the arrival of Kevin Nash and Scott Hall in WCW, with their hostile invasion storyline helping Nitro achieve strong ratings and generate a huge buzz in the industry. Never one to shy away from an opportunity for self-promotion, Hogan saw the gravy train about to leave the station and hopped on board at the last minute. Bischoff had been promising a third man to join the duo at Bash At The Beach, so Hogan asked him, "Brother, who's the third man?" Bischoff told him he didn't know, to which Hogan replied, "I think you're looking at him."

However, Hogan still had his reservations and went back and forth on the matter, unsure up until the last minute about whether he could really go through with rejecting the persona that had made him a millionaire and the most famous wrestler in the world. Sensing that Hogan was a risk, Bischoff concocted a back-up plan. He would ask another life-long babyface, Sting, to step into the breach if necessary. Sting was a strong candidate. He was essentially the face of WCW, the one man who had never worked for Vince McMahon, and for him to turn heel would be a big deal. He was reluctant when he heard the idea – despite realising that his meandering career would benefit from an association with the hottest act in wrestling – but he agreed to do it if that was what Bischoff wanted. Eventually, despite last minute concerns that he would not go through with it, Hogan executed the turn and Hollywood Hogan and the nWo were born.

Sting turning would still have been huge news and he would have made a great leader of the nWo, but it is unlikely to have had anywhere near the same impact as Hulk Hogan. Instead, Sting would likely have been forced to lay down for Hogan, killing the angle stone dead before it even really got off the ground.

STING WAS NEARLY "THE THIRD MAN"

WRESTLEMANIA III'S "PLAN B"

Hulk Hogan versus Andre The Giant at *WrestleMania III* is rightly regarded as a seminal moment in mainstream professional wrestling. It is perhaps the most famous match of all time, featuring one of the most iconic moments in WWE history when Hogan slammed Andre and pinned him to retain his championship. WWF lore would be very different without that moment, yet, it nearly didn't happen at all.

Andre Roussimoff was done with professional wrestling by the middle of 1986. He'd requested time off from the WWF after *WrestleMania 2*, and was written out of storylines by the end of April. It was partly because he'd landed the role of Fezzik in the cult classic movie *The Princess Bride*, a role that would later help to define him in the mainstream public consciousness away from wrestling.

The other factor was Andre's increasing health problems. A sufferer of acromegaly (colloquially known as "gigantism"), Andre was about to turn forty (an age doctors said he would never reach) and he was in constant pain, slowing down to the point that he could barely move, be it inside or outside of the ring. Andre knew it was time to hang up his boots and intended to quietly walk away from the spotlight with little fanfare.

It was Vince McMahon himself who persuaded Andre to return. Flying to London where *The Princess Bride* was shooting, McMahon filled Andre in on what he had concocted for *WrestleMania III*: the biggest match in the history of American professional wrestling, Hulk Hogan vs. Andre the Giant. There are few people as persuasive as Vincent Kennedy McMahon when he wants something, and Andre was back in the WWF by June.

However, even though Andre had agreed to the plan, the matter of whether he would be healthy enough to compete at the supershow was still a pressing concern. In case Andre was forced to pull out, the WWF came up with a Plan B. His name was Paul Orndorff. A genuine hard-man of the old school, with a great look and ability to match, Orndorff had made big money working with Hogan in 1986 and 1987, with one house show in Toronto where they we billed as the main event selling out to the tune of 74,000 people. The astronomical number caused the WWF to hurriedly throw together a strong line-up and sent video cameras to film the action for a VHS release. Orndorff and Hogan was a hot program, no doubt about it.

Their feud, evenly matched for the most part, had ended with the traditional 1980s blow-off of a cage match, but one with a finish designed to leave loose ends. Should Andre have to pull out then Orndorff would have seamlessly slotted in, and chance are given their past record drawing everywhere they went, the Pontiac Silverdome would have been sold out just the same, with a whole new iconic moment cementing itself permanently in the minds of wrestling fans worldwide.

Unfortunately for Orndorff, Andre did make the match, cruelly leaving him without a match and without a bonus on the biggest payday of the year. While Orndorff was undoubtedly a huge star anyway, a match with Hogan on the biggest show of all time would have cemented his status as one of the greats, but instead he is considered to be someone who was on the verge of superstardom but never quite made it to that elite level.

CHYNA - WWE CHAMPION

Few would argue that Chyna is not one of the most dominant female athletes in WWE history. Her intense physicality all but decimated the female roster with frightening ease, so much so that WWE were keen to challenge gender prejudice by having Chyna wrestle and defeat male talent. Her feuds with Jeff Jarrett and Chris Jericho along with her pioneering reign as Intercontinental Champion stand as testament that WWE once weren't afraid to take calculated risks. However, the biggest risk in relation to Chyna was actually set to take place before her IC run. Amazingly, there was briefly a plan in place for Chyna to become the first female wrestler to win the coveted WWE Championship at *SummerSlam '99*. In the build-up to the event she became the number one contender, and it looked like 'Stone Cold' Steve Austin versus Chyna was set to close WWE's third biggest PPV of the year. But it was little more than a red herring designed by Vince Russo to throw viewers off the scent about the WWF's direction, though he did admit that if it was down to him he would have done the match and put Chyna over. Progressive booking, shock TV or just typical Russo madness? Either way, it never happened and Chyna had to settle for the IC Title instead.

WHO KILLED MR. MCMAHON?

Had the Chris Benoit tragedy not happened in June 2007, one of the most daring wrestling storylines ever was planned to unfold for the duration of the year. When Mr. McMahon was seemingly blown up and killed in his limousine following an angle on *Raw*, the question of "Who killed Mr. McMahon?" was to be left unanswered for months.

The plan was for an investigation to slowly uncover evidence that proved that Mr. McMahon's murderer was in fact orchestrated by Linda McMahon, who would subsequently be arrested. A video of her late husband's final will and testament would then be discovered and shown on *Raw*, where McMahon bequeathed the entire WWE to his illegitimate son, Mr. Kennedy.

Kennedy was to become the number one heel in the promotion and would use his executive powers to place himself in both the WWE and World Heavyweight Title pictures. Meanwhile, Triple H and Stephanie McMahon were planned to reveal their (kayfabe) second consensual marriage that would allow Triple H to challenge Kennedy for ownership of WWE.

The feud between Triple H and Kennedy was scheduled to play out until *WrestleMania* culminating in a main event match that would be won by Triple H, who would then be considered the undisputed owner of the WWE. At which point, Mr. McMahon would return and reveal that he had faked his own death and planted evidence to incriminate his wife for his murder so that he could give WWE to his "true son."

The Benoit tragedy forced WWE to abandon these plans when the COO of the company had to break kayfabe and address fans on *Raw*, killing the story. Besides, it would be in very poor taste to run a murder storyline after the real-life horrific murders that had taken place in the Benoit home. The angle was scrapped completely and never mentioned again.

JOHN CENA KILLED THE NEXUS

In 2010, WWE's stale product became interesting again with the emergence of The Nexus. Led by Wade Barrett, the group of (pre-Full Sail) NXT rookies emulated the tried and tested "outsider" gimmick that had worked so well for the nWo fourteen years earlier (and the WCW/ECW Alliance, which was not so successful). As The Nexus grew in popularity, WWE developed a *SummerSlam* pay-per-view main event pitting The Nexus against Team WWE in a fourteen-man elimination match.

The original plan was to continue the develop of The Nexus by having them win the match cleanly, a result which would continue their momentum for the medium to long term. However, according to Edge and Chris Jericho—who both participated in the match as members of Team WWE—John Cena lobbied to have the match end with Team WWE prevailing over the renegade septet.

According to them, Cena wanted to be the last member of Team WWE against the remaining members of Team Nexus, Wade Barrett and Justin Gabriel. He then wanted to receive a DDT at ringside before somehow resurging in the ring to eliminate both. Which is exactly how the bout ended up playing out.

Jericho and Edge both disagreed with Cena, believing that The Nexus should have won, particularly as they had so much heat and were clearly over with the fans. Cena regretted changing the finish as soon as he walked back through the curtain following the match. But all of the regret in the world was not going to make any difference. All of the heat that had surrounded the faction prior to *SummerSlam* had completely dissipated following the event.

Imagine if the original plans for Team Nexus to walk out of *SummerSlam* as victors went ahead unchanged. Perhaps the faction would have been revered as a modern day now. Unfortunately, following Cena's intervention The Nexus fizzled away, its members relegated to mid-card jobbers and its leader forced to endure multiple gimmick changes and fruitless WWE pushes. A senseless waste of talent.

JERICHO WANTED TO TATTOO PUNK

Vince McMahon's opinion of whether blood-letting should be part of wrestling varies depending on who his sponsors are at the time, but in 2012 he was definitely of the mind-set that spilling claret was absolutely outlawed on his broadcasts.

It was the prospect of a tiny amount of the red stuff that put him off an odd little storyline pitched by Chris Jericho in 2012. As part of his feud with the heavily-tattooed C.M. Punk, Jericho wanted to legitimately tattoo the 'Straight Edge Superstar', and Vince was initially keen. Then out of leftfield he turned on the idea.

According to Jericho. "I think someone got in his ear that there was going to be blood. Plus, Vince said he has a million tattoos. Well, it doesn't matter if he has a million tattoos. What if I tattoo my initials on him FOR REAL? Punk was saying let's do this for real and that is like being violated.

"I was begging Vince for us to do the tattoo angle; someone had told Vince that tattoos will create blood and Vince got scared. Plus, no one would see it for the reason to describe but he doesn't have tattoos so he doesn't get it.

"He came up with the idea that Punk's dad has problems with alcohol and you think he wouldn't go for it but to Punk's credit, he went for it. I don't know if he had issues with his family and he wanted to take it out with them and I don't think he even told his dad about it."

That Vince refused to do a potentially memorable angle such as that because of a trickle of blood seems ridiculous in hindsight given he authorised far bloodier displays in the years that followed. Had the tattoo angle been proposed five years earlier or a few years later, chances are it would have happened. Instead, Punk remains with only a "million" tattoos rather than one-million-and-one.

SUMMERSLAM '92 REBOOKED

Back in the 1990s, the WWF would tape three weeks' worth of weekly television shows Superstars and Wrestling Challenge over a single weekend, which would air over the following few weeks. These tended to give a good indication of where the company was going with its storylines, sometimes even giving away what was going to happen on upcoming pay-per-view events. In the tapings held after WrestleMania VIII, storylines were put in place for August's SummerSlam four months later. The original card read as follows:

WWF Championship
Randy Savage © vs. Ric Flair

WWF Intercontinental Championship
Bret Hart © vs. Shawn Michaels

WWF Tag Team Championship
Money Inc. © vs. The Natural Disasters

The Ultimate Warrior vs. Papa Shango

The Undertaker vs. The Berzerker

Tatanka vs. Rick Martel

The British Bulldog vs. Repo Man

While none of the matches were ever officially announced, it was clear from the booking at the television tapings that this was the direction the WWF were going in. Angles shot included Papa Shango cursing The Ultimate Warrior with voodoo and causing him to leak black ooze from his forehead and vomit, The Berzerker attempting to stab The Undertaker with his sword, Rick Martel stole the feathers from Tatanka's sacred headdress, and the Repo Man stole an angle made famous four years earlier by Tom Prichard and Dirty White Boy in Continental when he hanged The British Bulldog with a tow rope in a graphic and often-forgotten angle on Wrestling Challenge.

Everything was geared towards SummerSlam, which at that point was scheduled to be held in Washington, but plans changed when Vince McMahon was given the chance to bring the event to England's 80,000 capacity Wembley Stadium. With the company enduring its worst spell since Vince took over the reins from his father in 1983, he was eager to take the opportunity to present the WWF as a successful, thriving entity. Knowing he would sell out in England, where conversely the WWF was enjoying its peak, McMahon moved the show.

The change in venue necessitated a rejigging of the card, with McMahon shifting English native The British Bulldog into a match with his brother-in-law Bret Hart for the Intercontinental Championship. That was not the only match McMahon changed. With SummerSlam now taking place in a huge stadium, he felt the show needed a main event that was worthy of the setting. Feeling a Flair-Savage rerun was not going to generate the level of interest required to make the show a success, McMahon instead turned to The Ultimate Warrior, scrapping his unpopular program with Papa Shango and thrusting him into the title picture. As a result, Flair was dropped from the card completely. Vince continued to wield the axe, and by the time he was finished every match on the show was changed from the original plan.

Not to say they did not still happen though. Savage and Flair wrestled for the title on television in September a few weeks after SummerSlam, with Flair winning the belt. Michaels and Hart main evented Survivor Series in November, The Natural Disasters defeated Money Inc. to win the tag belts on a Worcester house show in July, Warrior teamed with Undertaker to defeated Shango and Berzerker in a series of bouts on the road which served to kill two feuds with one stone, and Tatanka battled Martel at Survivor Series.

One of the brightest stars of the 1980s, Magnum TA – so named because of a mild resemblance to superstar actor Tom Selleck, whose PI show Magnum was hot at the time – never made it to the megastar level that everyone in the industry had prophesied for him due to a tragic accident.

Towards the end of 1985 while working for WCW forerunner Jim Crockett Promotions, Magnum was fresh off hugely successful feud with Ric Flair over the NWA World Heavyweight Championship, testing the waters for an eventual full-blown title run.

The message was clear: Magnum TA was over as JCP's top babyface, and being JCP's top babyface essentially made him the NWA's top babyface. The word was unofficial, but everyone knew Magnum was a lock to dethrone Flair and win the title at *Starrcade '86* in November.

Magnum was about to embark on a length title run, a reign which would cement him as one of the biggest stars in the world at only twenty-seven years old. Then came the day of October 14, 1986. Having wrestled in Greenville, South Carolina the night before against Jimmy Garvin, Magnum was returning home prior to a TV taping in Colombia, SC, when he lost control of his high-powered Porsche and hydroplaned in the wet conditions and smashed into a telegraph pole. The accident was bad. Magnum survived, but he was fortunate to do so. However, it came at a cost. In the accident two of Magnum's vertebrae "practically exploded", leaving him paralysed for many months and his wrestling career over.

Magnum's incredible physical condition saved his life and eventually allowed him to walk again, but the damage was too severe for him to ever return to the ring. Magnum never wrestled again following the accident and pro wrestling moved on without him, leaving him as one of wrestling's most tragic "What if?" tales.

THE TRAGEDY OF MAGNUM TA

THE GOLDBERG BLUEPRINT

During the glory years of World Championship Wrestling, the promotion was not regarded as a company that created their own stars. The organisation did have their hallmark names, like Ric Flair, Diamond Dallas Page and Sting, but there were precious few legitimate main eventers produced during WCW's peak. Eric Bischoff preferred to use ready-made stars who had made their names in the WWF or ECW, luring them to the company with the promise of guaranteed money and a gentle schedule. One of the few who did come through the ranks and graduated from WCW's training school the Power Plant became an absolute phenomenon.

Bill Goldberg almost-instantly role to stardom in late-1997. Following his television debut against Hugh Morrus on the September 22nd episode of Nitro, Goldberg began ripping through all and sundry on the roster. Suddenly, it became clear that Goldberg was on quite the winning streak, and fans began keeping track of his victories. WCW earnestly encouraged this, realising they had a star in the making on their hands.

The streak lasted a remarkable 173 straight victories, which included a United States Championship win over Raven on Nitro, and then the peak of his career; dethroning WCW World Heavyweight Champion Hollywood Hogan in front of 40,000 at the Georgia Dome on July 6, 1998. It wasn't until Starrcade in December of that year that WCW ended Goldberg's winning run. The man to do it was none other than WCW booker Kevin Nash, who deemed himself worthy of ending Goldberg's streak and writing his name into the record books. Fans were furious, though Nash remains unrepentant, claiming he was just as over as Goldberg at the time and he hardly benefited from the win because he dropped the title to Hogan a few weeks later as part of the infamous Finger-poke Of Doom angle.

Due to the success of Bill Goldberg, WCW were keen to follow the template of his success. Midcard workers such as Bryan 'Wrath' Clarke were put on winning runs with the hope being that they could emulate Goldberg, but the impact was nowhere near the same. Even Sid Vicious was handed the winning streak gimmick in 1999, largely as a tool to begin a feud with Goldberg, though that didn't get him far either.

There were many other attempts to ape Goldberg's run in WCW and WWE, but they all ended up petering out in the same way. This proved that it was not simply the steak which got Goldberg over, but his natural charisma, unmatched intensity and cool, mysterious aura. He was truly one of a kind.

THE MYSTERY OF GTV

WWE's list of mysteriously dropped storylines and gimmicks is a long and colourful one. In 1999, one of the biggest onscreen mysteries was the identity of the person responsible for hidden camera exposé piece GTV, which aired each week on Raw and revealed candid footage of WWE Superstars in embarrassing situations.

It lasted for months, with the idea seemingly that the person responsible would eventually be outed, leading to a series of matches with someone who had been humiliated by GTV revelations. But then it just ended out of nowhere without any pay-off.

Originally it was going to be Goldust, but he was released before the angle reached a conclusion. According to him: "It was for me. In recent years I've tried to bring that back to the table with Vince but he's like, 'No, no. We're not going to use that right now.' Now, it's kind of gotten lost in the shuffle. The majority of people wouldn't remember GTV."

According to Chris Jericho, the man to replace Goldust as the brains behind GTV was supposed to be MTV prankster Tom Green. Remember him? His fame was tied to basically demeaning himself for attention, so the candid camera situation would—sort of—fit. Unfortunately for Green, the gimmick died when Vince McMahon realised what everyone else knew already, as Jericho confirmed: "Tom Green used to film stuff you know, pranks, stuff and all that sh*t. Then what happened was they started planting the seeds for GTV and Vince actually saw Tom Green's stuff and said, 'This guy is not funny.' Done."

THE REAL KANE

In 2006 an unmasked Kane came face to face with a fully masked 'Imposter' Kane, a storyline penned following speculation that Kane's portrayer Glenn Jacobs was contemplating retirement. As a result, WWE—not wanting to completely abandon the character—decided to create a facsimile of Kane based on his look at the time of his memorable 1997 debut. Having Kane #2 masked and fully suited also afforded the man behind the mask, Drew Hankinson (later Festus and Luke Gallows), the opportunity to perform the role with anonymity in case it flopped, thus not derailing the rest of his career. The plan was to have Imposter Kane eventually revealed as the "real" Kane, with the explanation being that Glenn Jacobs had imprisoned him for years before stealing his identity. The plans were dropped when the storyline failed to get over with fans, and Jacobs decided to hold off his retirement for another decade. Had Jacobs decided to take his gold watch, we may have spent the next ten years watching Hankinson as the masked Kane on WWE TV today.

THE GAME CHANGER

It's no secret that Triple H has used his stroke to influence booking plans throughout his career. On several occasions he even engineered changes to *WrestleMania* main events. At *WrestleMania X-8* the main event was originally set to feature The Rock-Hulk Hogan showdown for the ages, but 'The Game' successfully lobbied for the running order to change in favour of giving his heatless WWF Championship match with Chris Jericho top billing instead. As a result, following the Hogan-Rock match an emotionally-spent audience was forced to endure an anti-climactic replacement, which ultimately ended the event on a rather underwhelming note.

A year later at *WrestleMania XIX* he was at it again, changing the outcome of his World Heavyweight Championship match with Booker T. The original plan was for Booker to win and become World Heavyweight Champion, but Hunter convinced management that it was the wrong move and successfully had the match changed so that he would retain the gold.

He was at it again six years later at *WrestleMania XXV* when he insisted that his WWE Championship match with Randy Orton headlined a show that featured company icons Shawn Michaels and The Undertaker colliding. Upon seeing the two legends assemble a classic, Hunter turned to Orton and simply said, "We're f*cked." He was right. In every case, Hunter would have been better off just leaving the booking well alone.

KIZARNY AND VINCE THE CLOWN

Having tried out for the WWE a number of times, Canadian weirdo (by his own insistence) Nick Cvjetkovich finally earned a development contract with in 2007, then reported to FCW where he wrestled as Sinn Bowdee.

Believing that he had potential, WWE promoted him to the main roster, allowing his creative input on a new oddball gimmick known as Kizarny. The name was an inside reference to the mostly obsolete practice of speaking "carny", with the name Kizarny the carny pronunciation of the word carny. Yes, they thought they were hilarious.

Despite weeks of vignettes promoting him Kizarny was a bust almost immediately. Following his debut match with MVP in October 2008 he was quickly moved into the background, then released from his contract five months later.

According to Kizarny—in a WWE Universe blog that was quickly removed from the official site when he was dropped, and in subsequent interviews—he had pitched multiple ideas for his direction. The most outlandish of all was a suggestion for a new tag team featuring him and Vince McMahon, only with McMahon donning face-paint and silly hair as the latest incarnation of Doink the Clown!

Unsurprisingly, that pitch didn't exactly land.

Given Kizarny's other "skills"—outlined in a slightly bitter interview a while after his dismissal—it's not at all surprising WWE were so quick to turn their backs on their once valued idea:

"...I do know my craft and I am a hell-on-wheels competitor that would give any opponent a run for his money... How many wrestlers do you know that can drink boiling water with thumbtacks and razor blades, have darts thrown at their body, nail a nail to their nose, juggle live rabbits, shatter concrete blocks with their skulls, impale themselves with shark hooks and regurgitate rubber chickens?!?! Let's see John whop-dee-doo Cena do that!!!"

EL MATADOR - WWF CHAMPION

In 1992 the WWF was coming under fire from all quarters due to a series of scandals that were tarnishing the company's family-friendly image. Principal amongst them was the allegation that all WWF wrestlers were using and abusing steroids. With government officials sniffing around and looking for any shred of evidence they could find to hang McMahon out to dry, the WWF chairman was forced into action. He quickly severed ties with anyone on his roster who was blatantly using performance enhancing drugs to shape their physiques, a list which included notable stars such as Hulk Hogan, The British Bulldog and The Ultimate Warrior.

In order to project a strong public image, McMahon realised that his WWF Champion needed to be a symbol of the new, clean, WWF. Or to put it another way, they could not look like jacked up 'roid freaks. McMahon drew up a shortlist of names who could potentially hold the coveted title and discussed them with his closest aides. Names such as Randy Savage and Rick Martel were considered but dismissed because of their ages, Undertaker was not an option because he was considered a sideshow attraction who did not need the title, Shawn Michaels had only recently turned heel and was still finding his feet in the role, so he was deemed not ready.

The list came down to Bret Hart and Tito Santana - who was wrestling under his hackneyed bullfighter gimmick El Matador. Santana had been a consistent soldier for McMahon for over a decade and could always be relied upon to deliver solid performances. However, McMahon felt that he too was past his best and would struggle to generate the fan support someone in that positioned needed. He eventually passed up on Santana in favour of the younger, more popular Bret Hart. Santana did not learn how close he was to the pinnacle of the WWF until the day he handed in his notice the following year.

As he recalls, Pat Patterson told him that evening, "It was down to you and Bret for the strap." Santana was stunned to hear that revelation, but played it off light-heartedly. "Gee Pat, I wish you'd never told me that." The wrestling world would have been a very different place had Santana been given the title instead of Bret Hart. He likely would have headlined the following year's WrestleMania, though it is unlikely that his appalling win-loss record at the big show would have improved much if he had. Whoever had the belt would have dropped it to Yokozuna that day in Nevada.

MR. G AND THE G-SPOTS

In 1997, Tod Gordon's association with ECW was controversially tenuous. Despite being part of a powerful clique backstage with Sabu, The Sandman and Bill Alfonso, Gordon's backstage clout—merely ceremonial after selling his stake in the company to Paul Heyman in 1995—wasn't as significant as he wanted. Gordon wanted his role as ECW Commissioner to be expanded into a more prominent character, but Paul Heyman resisted, just as Gordon had resisted Heyman's urging to expand ECW. His plan was to either become The Sandman's manager or to manage two female wrestlers. The latter gimmick would have seen the three adopt the gimmick of Mr. G And The G-Spots—individually called Peaches and Cream. Given the obvious sexual undertones it was the sort of idea that would have been right at home in ECW, but Heyman refused to let Gordon expand his role.

SABLE AND THE HUMMER

Make no mistake about it, Sable was one of the WWF's biggest stars in the Attitude Era. It should be no surprise then that WCW made an immediate play to sign her when she departed the WWF in 1999. Her first WCW appearance was as a member of the *Nitro* crowd, just days after her WWF exit. She was legally not allowed to appear as she was still under a WWF no-compete clause, but WCW argued that she was that she was just there as a fan. Regardless, the WWF's lawyers warned against using her again or they would sue. That warning ended up nixing plans to reveal Sable as the driver of a Hummer that had crashed into Kevin Nash's limo. WCW even hinted that she was the attacker, then never revealed the driver. Whatever plans WCW had for Sable, they never ended up seeing the light of day, and the Hummer whodunit angle remains one of wrestling's great unsolved mysteries.

TANK ABBOTT - WCW CHAMPION

If there's one thing that can be said in favour of this entry, it's that former UFC star Tank Abbott was at least physically involved in the WCW product. Unlike, say, Judy Bagwell, Abbott actually took bumps and competed in matches. Even so, he did it to little fanfare from fans, failing to truly get over as a professional wrestler. Tank simply didn't grasp the basic mechanics of a wrestling bout. Nevertheless, Vince Russo pitched an idea to make Tank Abbot WCW's World Champion. The promotion was scrambling for ideas to fill up time on the upcoming *Souled Out* Pay-Per-View in January, 2000 and one of Russo's big proposals was making the mid-card shoot fighter the top titleholder. The writer's logic was that because of Tank's legitimate fighting background he could have beaten up many wrestlers on the roster for real. Not that fan's cared about that. If WCW had made Abbott champion, viewers would have tuned out of WCW far earlier than they did. The idea was enough to convince acting WCW President Bill Busch—who knew nothing about wrestling—that Russo was out of his mind, and he fired him shortly afterwards.

KEVIN DUNN'S INFLUENCE

In the long history of WWE gimmicks, one of the most startling revelations is how many hugely successful angles were initially met with derision or a lack of enthusiasm by hierarchy. Take, for instance, the infamous Single White Female story involving Trish Stratus and Mickie James. It was a resounding success for both, but infamous WWE producer Kevin Dunn fought tooth and nail to have it squashed: According to the man who penned the angle, Alex Greenfield, "He fought us every week. Show was heavy? KD wanted to cut Trish/Mickie. Temple of Trish segment? KD argued that we needed more action and people would get bored. Lesbian kiss? 'Trish has gotta like it!' Every single element, he wanted both protagonist and villain to be sexier and stupider."

HALE BABY

Emory Hale was a pet project of 'The Mouth Of The South' Jimmy Hart in WCW. Much like many others in the company over the years, Hale was paid a lot of money for doing very little in return. The promotion tried several times to turn him into a star, but he was never really a success. One of the most notable gimmicks the man was given was so short-lived that most fans barely remember it.

In 2000, Hale was turned into 'The Machine'. The idea was that he'd be so physically imposing that fans would surely react to him. Just like Goldberg. To be on the safe side, he was placed under a mask, one which oddly made the man look like little more than a gimp. Quite literally, The Machine wore a gimp mask to the ring, something which was never really explained by WCW announcers. In his debut match on Thunder, the man faced Diamond Dallas Page, who was at the time a rising star in the promotion. Quickly improving inside the ring, Page would later become an impressive late-bloomer, already into his 40's by the time he won the WCW World Title in 1999.

During the bout, fans witnessed one of the most unintentionally comedic spots Monday Nitro had ever seen. Standing atop one of the corner turnbuckles, Hale was supposed to be crotched by Page, but the spot was horrifically blown. In fairness to Hale, DDP also played his part in the terrible sequence fans witnessed on live television.

Shaking the ropes next to The Machine, Page watched in disbelief as Hale stood up, screamed, and jumped onto the ropes all on his own. The spot looked terrible, and it was hard for fans to take the already-bland Machine character seriously afterwards. Hale had been in line for a major push in the company prior to the match, but this uninspiring performance really hurt his chances.

WCW didn't release him from contract, and instead repackaged him as simply Hail and then later Hale Baby, a confusing gimmick designed to make him a babyface. Shouting at opponents, 'You're going to Hale (Hell)', his foe would then – hopefully - be met by a cry of, 'Baby!' from the audience. That idea didn't catch on either. At all. Any dreams of turning Hale into a main event star were quickly abolished. Unfortunately, Hale never did make it as a superstar. He sadly passed away in 2006 as a result of long-term kidney problems at the age of just 35-years old.

BRIAN PILLMAN WAS GOING TO STEAL GOLDUST'S WIFE

Everyone loves a good romantic entanglement storyline. Or at least, WWE creative seem to think so. Apparently, there's something about muscle-bound posturing that makes stealing each other's love interests an important way to assert machismo. That's how it almost went for Brian Pillman and Goldust in 1997. Had the former not died just prior to the *In Your House: Badd Blood* PPV (on which they were scheduled to face each other), the pair's XXX Files storyline would have ended with Pillman stealing Goldust's manager—and Pillman's real-life ex—Terri Runnels (Which, in reality, Goldust was genuinely upset about). Having been "won" by Pillman for thirty days, Runnels was set to return to Goldust and the pair were going to renew their vows in the ring. As with all wrestling weddings it was set to end in tears with Pillman crashing the ceremony and Terri admitting she had fallen in love with him. She would then run off with him—in her wedding dress—leaving her husband and child behind.

CHRISTIAN WAS RESPONSIBLE FOR JEFF HARDY'S "ACCIDENTS"

Despite the poetic revelation that Matt Hardy was behind a number of mysterious accidents befalling his brother Jeff (including the tasteless use of Jeff's real-life house fire for the angle), the revelation at the end of that storyline wasn't actually intended to lead to a family affair. Originally, Christian was supposed to be the orchestrator, so instead of Matt helping Edge steal Jeff's WWE Championship at *Royal Rumble*, Edge's former tag partner Christian—who was carrying the struggling ECW brand—would have intervened, likely leading to a series of Edge & Christian vs. Hardy Boyz matches. When the plans leaked online WWE pulled the plug and changed tact, leaving Christian directionless.

RAVEN'S SEVEN DEADLY SINS

Having successfully built a persona based on Patrick Swayze's surfer criminal in *Point Break* and an iconic gothic poem, Raven was a well-established character prior to his arrival in the WWF. Unfortunately, the high-point of his run there came when he killed Perry Saturn's best friend Moppy (a mop). Shortly thereafter, the nihilistic multi-time Hardcore Champion was relegated to the status of jobber and mostly kept away from TV. After briefly flirting with announcing, he was given creative control to develop a gimmick based on the movie *Se7en*. His storyline would see him become a puppet master and punish other wrestlers for breaking the seven deadly sins, culminating in a feud with Matt Hardy over Lita. Unfortunately for Raven, management pulled the plug shortly after it started, citing a lack of interest from the crowd. More likely it was down to Vince McMahon's directive that Raven not be pushed, down to his own personal dislike of the man behind the character—Scott Levy—for having led his son Shane McMahon astray in the mid-90s.

VINCE RUSSO'S TNA INVASIONS

In 2014, Vince Russo was brought on board "secretly" by TNA to help stop their inevitable march towards oblivion. As part of that objective, he pitched that old wrestling trope—an invasion angle—which he hoped would help turn the company's fortunes around. "At the time, Spike TV had yet to make the decision on whether, or not, they were going to offer the company another contract, as the existing one was about to expire. As the Hulkster would say, speculation was running wild throughout the Internet Wrestling Community as to the future of TNA on Spike TV." Russo took it upon himself to formulate an angle where other wrestling brands would try and take advantage of the uncertainty regarding TNA's future by showing up on *Impact* to try and convince Spike TV to give them the slot instead. He wanted ROH and Jeff Jarrett's GFW to "invade", but when his idea was mostly ignored over concerns that the talent wasn't available to pull in the money and attention, he gave up.

MARK HENRY WAS GOING TO BREAK THE STREAK

According to former writer Alex Greenfield, Vince McMahon considered having Mark Henry end The Undertaker's streak at *WrestleMania*. Greenfield admitted that the 'Mania bookings were based on pitches suggested by the creative team, which were then also ran by 'Taker himself, and that McMahon came up with the Henry idea: "Several times through the process, Vince played with the idea of Mark actually taking the Streak, though none of us ever pitched that to my knowledge. Vince is very much the booker in the classic wrestling sense."

At *SummerSlam '92* the original booking for the WWF Championship match between Randy Savage and The Ultimate Warrior was for the latter to go over for the title, following a heel turn. Warrior—a babyface throughout his career as the face-paint-covered superhero—was set to join forces with Ric Flair and Mr. Perfect, selling out in exchange for their services in helping him defeat Savage. Warrior would have then gone on to work a programme with Bret Hart culminating in a match at *Survivor Series* that he would win, before dropping the title to Hart at *WrestleMania IX*. However, Warrior refused to turn to the dark side and plans were cancelled. Warrior was gone from the company three months later.

THE ULTIMATE WARRIOR'S HEEL TURN

It's startling to consider, but Buff Bagwell's non-wrestling mother is in the history books as a former WCW Tag Team Champion. Mercifully, Judy didn't actually wrestle to win the gold. Rick Steiner had already won the titles by himself and was allowed to pick any partner of his choosing to co-hold the titles with. In a segment that baffled everybody watching, Steiner plumped for Buff Bagwell's momma. Unbelievably, prior to this title-killing debacle, Judy had actually been earmarked for another run as champion. This time, her tag-team partner would have been her own son. It's unconfirmed as to whether or not Judy would have involved herself physically during these matches, but regardless of that the idea was obviously ridiculous. The angle was proposed as a way to generate sympathy for Buff, who had suffered a serious neck injury during a match against Steiner in 1998, and was all set to return as an avenging babyface. WCW hoped to make him a sympathetic character that fans could get behind, with the theory being that having his loving mother by his side would endear him to the audience. Quite exactly how this was going to do that is anyone's guess, especially from an audience used to cheering heels the nWo and throwing garbage into the ring when they did not like something. Somewhere in the WCW creative office a rare bout of common sense took hold and plans for the Bagwells tandem was dropped. Instead Buff returned to the ring as a heel, delivering a battering to Steiner upon his return and siding with Rick's real life brother and fellow heel Scott Steiner instead. Curiously, life imitated art somewhat when Bagwell reached the WWF in 2001 when Buff proved to his stunned new employers that he really was a mummy's boy. Following some backstage altercations with other members of the locker room, Buff decided to call in sick, a big no-no in the WWF. To make matters worse, he did not do it himself, he had Judy call Head of Talent Relations Jim Ross with the news. After taking the call, a shocked Ross told her, "I'd also like to remind you, Mrs. Bagwell, that if you ever want to call here again and speak with me, I'll be happy to speak with you about anything in the world but your son - because this is the last conversation you and I will ever have about your boy, because he's a man. He should be calling me, not you."

JUDY BAGWELL - MULTI-TIME CHAMPION

THE LONG-TERM PLAN FOR THE NWO

By far, the New World Order faction was the best idea WCW vice president Eric Bischoff ever had. Even though Nitro first went head to head with WWF Raw in September 1995, it wasn't until the advent of the nWo in July 1996 that the program really started to catch fire. When it did, WCW was untouchable for a spell, and became arguably the hottest wrestling company on the planet.

By January 1997, Bischoff was utterly drunk on the success that the nWo had generated for WCW. Such was the renegade faction's seemingly unstoppable momentum that he had a brainwave: he would give the nWo their own show. His plan was to hand over Nitro to the nWo and have WCW control the new Thursday night show Thunder that he was negotiating with TBS executives. As a trial run to gauge how successful the nWo would be as a breakaway brand, Bischoff created a pay-per-view based entirely around the group.

To capture the essence of the New World Order, Bischoff instructed his production team to create a complete different feel to the broadcast, which had been named *Souled Out*. The usually vibrant presentation was instead bathed only in black and white, the colours of the nWo. WCW performers on the card were stripped of entrance music and ring introductions, instead mocked and insulted by a disembodied pro-nWo announcer as they traversed the aisle. Bischoff handled commentating duties himself, alongside fellow nWo member Ted DiBiase, and the pair spent the majority of the broadcast ignoring the in-ring action in favour of discussing motorcycles, and stroking Hogan's ego.

"*Souled Out* was designed to be the nWo's version of what a pay-per-view should look like - an attempt to give pay-per-view a different feel," defends Bischoff. "Everything about it was designed to reflect the renegade, counterculture anarchy that defined nWo. It had a stark, industrial feel, and we tried to do things in keeping with that.

"At the same time, I hoped to explore and possibly lay the foundations for separating WCW into separate brands: the mainstream of older WCW brand and the rebel nWo. Each would have its own roster of wrestlers and, eventually, its own show. That way, I could have my own war. I knew competition was the key to our success. Us versus them was the formula that had gotten us to the top of the ratings. Everyone had always fantasised about an event pitting the WWF and WCW wrestlers - a Super Bowl, if you will. That was never going to happen. But I thought that, by creating two brands, I would get as close as possible. We were so far ahead of the WWF that they were not even really competition, at least not in my mind."

The whole experience was unquestionably different, but within a few minutes the novelty value wore off and the joke began to wear thin. The 5,120 capacity crowd at the Five Seasons Center in Cedar Rapids, IA soon realised that this was not a professional wrestling show, it was a three-hour long ego trip. Dave Meltzer wrote in his *Wrestling Observer*:

Souled Out, which came off to outsiders as the brainchild of someone intoxicated by his own success to the point of all perspective being lost, was the single worst PPV show in the history of pro wrestling. You may call it the night that the nWo gimmick was fully exposed. Maybe it'll even go down as a turning point in an ever changing wrestling war at the very worst. There have been shows where the quality of the matches were worse, although this would be a bad show by that criterion. There have been shows with less heat and worse atmosphere, although this would be a bad show by those criteria as well. But there has never been a show with such poor announcing and outside wrestling skits, combined with the bad wrestling, lack of heat and bad atmosphere.

The pay-per-view buyrate numbers told the story. *Souled Out* pulled a 0.47 buyrate, or approximately half what WCW's previous event *Starrcade* had drawn in December. It was proof that while the nWo were the hottest thing on free television each week, as a stand-along brand that could sell tickets, they were not at the level Bischoff had pegged them to be.

"The numbers told me that we hadn't built the nWo up yet to the point where it could sustain its own weekly show," he says, "As strong as the concept had been up to this point, we didn't quite have the infrastructure in terms of story and talent to sustain it. The buzz was starting to weaken."

THE ORIGINAL PLAN FOR WRESTLEMANIA XXX

In 2013 Daniel Bryan was the most popular wrestler in the world, the man wrestling fans of all ages had elected as their chosen one. However, WWE felt differently. Vince McMahon and his team felt that Bryan was too small, too pasty, too light, too… vegan, to ever make it as a main event calibre star. As heels Stephanie McMahon and Triple H were keen to point out at every opportunity, Bryan was, in their eyes, a "B+ player" rather than a bona fide headliner. Sick of being force-fed company approved top stars such as Randy Orton, Batista, and John Cena, the "WWE Universe" revolted.

Such was the strength of public backing for Bryan that fans began to intentionally sabotage angles he did not feature in. Mostly notably, the audience in Seattle on December 9, 2013 turned on a segment featuring a ring full of former WWE Champions that was designed to hype a match between Randy Orton and John Cena at that month's *TLC* pay-per-view. Dubbed "the biggest match of all-time", the clash between the two well-worn company kingpins was a unification match that would end WWE's ill-advised attempt to have two World Champions, restoring one champion at the head of WWE for the first time in over a decade. Fans did not care. They turned on the product, vociferously rejecting the match they were being sold and drowning out those speaking with non-step, deafening chants of "Daniel Bryan".

WWE ignored them. Vince McMahon wanted Randy Orton as his WWE Champion, and he already had his *WrestleMania XXX* main event set: Orton vs. Batista. The latter was booked to win the 2014 *Royal Rumble*, a result that everyone watching could see coming from a mile off. Again, they turned on what was placed in front of them. When Bryan was not even entered into the bout, fans booed heartily and began chanting his name, then gave winner Batista the same response. When CM Punk walked out of WWE the following day, nixing his planned match with Triple H at *WrestleMania*, WWE decided to finally capitalise on Bryan's fervent support and re-jigged the card. Through sheer fan will-power, he was afforded a spot in the main event of the biggest show of the year and was finally allowed his moment to shine when he tapped out Batista to lift the WWE World Heavyweight Championship.

RUSEV AND SUMMER'S WEDDING

Before Lana and Rusev mightily pissed off Vince McMahon by getting publicly engaged during the middle of a storyline where they were in relationships with other people, WWE had planned for Rusev to marry Summer Rae. They even set up a proposal, airing a segment the week before the real-life couple got engaged. Rusev and Lana disobeyed WWE's instructions to remain in character by posting on social media about their engagement, so Vince McMahon took out his frustration by having Rusev lose to Ryback clean on *Raw*. At that stage Summer Rae stepped into the ring and verbally demolished Rusev, before slapping him hard across the face. WWE then set about making sure both Rusev and Lana were repeatedly punished for daring to do something as reprehensible as fall in love.

MANKIND'S MOMMY

The WWF had lots of plans for Sable and Mankind in 1996. At *SummerSlam' 96* that much was hinted at when Foley interrupted a match between Goldust and Marc Mero to stalk Sable, without actually impacting the match. He then ran away, creepily, after calling her "Mommy". It would be easy to just dismiss it as typical Mankind weirdness, but it was actually destined to be an angle. That strange relationship would have started a feud between Mero and Mankind which would have culminated at *WrestleMania 13*. The idea was to then have Mankind, Sable and Paul Bearer (as well as Goldust and Marlena) band together as some sort of creepy, twisted family (presumably not voluntarily in Sable's case) akin to Jabba the Hutt and his posse of hangers on in *Return of the Jedi*. Unfortunately for the WWF creative team, Foley heard the planned endgame of the 'Mania match and rejected the entire angle, suggesting that if that was all he was being offered he'd prefer not to appear at *WrestleMania* at all. Mero ended up injured and off the show anyway, whereas Mankind was paired with Vader to take on Owen Hart and Davey Boy Smith, with the Sable association dropped entirely.

VINCE RUSSO'S WORKED SHOOTS

One of the strangest periods in wrestling history came when Vince Russo was the head of creative at WCW. By 1999, the company had become painfully stale. The magic of the nWo had all but disappeared, and management had done virtually nothing to prepare for that fact. The 'WCW' brand had been neglected, as Eric Bischoff dreamed of putting Vince McMahon and the WWF out of business.

Hopes were high that the incoming Russo would be the man to help WCW regain some focus. After all, many reasoned, he was the person taking credit for turning the ailing WWF's fortunes around in 1998. Those in charge at WCW certainly believed in Vince Russo, thinking him to be the one solely responsible for the advent of the WWF 'Attitude' Era. They failed to grasp that Russo was working underneath Vince McMahon and others in that company the whole time, and everything he did had to be approved before it reached television screens.

Giving Russo full control of WCW's product proved a complete disaster. Not only did he immediately completely disregarding the importance of the company's title belts, he also kick-started another trend that quickly turned away the core audience: 'shoot' storylines. With the rise of the internet, hardcore wrestling fans were more savvy and possessed more so-called insider knowledge than ever before. Russo mistakenly took this to mean that all fans would be interested in seeing 'shoot' storylines that abandoned the veil of kayfabe.

Unfortunately for him, most fans weren't remotely interested. In fact, most people were left confused when guys such as Buff Bagwell started jawing off during promos about doing jobs. Still, Russo persisted. He felt the idea would be ratings gold for WCW, and he planned to do much more of it. The WCW creative team therefore set about putting as much reality as they could into their storylines.

For every Bagwell shoot promo, and others such as Bill Goldberg 'not following the script' during a match with Scott Steiner, there were cancelled plans. That's a good thing too, because there's a chance WCW could have been killed a lot quicker than it was had Russo's worked shoot ideas come to fruition. Up and down the card, Russo wanted reality, despite ratings proving that the formula was not cutting it with fans. WCW wasn't great in 2000. In fact, it was frigging awful. But it could have been a lot worse if Russo had been given his way.

JOHN CENA'S RAP BATTLES

Having rescued his career by free-styling in front of Stephanie McMahon, John Cena's rap persona almost led to him squaring off with two hip hop legends. Cena issued an open invite to any celebrity to face him in a rap battle at *WrestleMania XIX*, which Jay Z accepted before being forced to cancel. As a substitute, Fabolous was drafted in, but he too had to pull out due to another engagement. Says Cena: "I regret that it didn't happen, because I'm a big hip-hop fan and I'm very rarely star struck. I not only admire Jay Z's music, but I look up to him as an entrepreneur. I was asked by a major journalist a question that you often get asked: 'If you could sit down at dinner with three people, who would it be?' I said, 'John D. Rockerfeller, FDR and Jay Z.'" It's unlikely it will happen again, given Cena's discomfort with some elements of his own image: "I sometimes feel awkward in denim shorts at 37. I would definitely feel awkward trying to spit street slang. That's something you do with the guys and you just try to hold your own. That's the extent of my hip-hop these days."

FEATURE:

BY DAN MADIGAN

A FEW THOUGHTS ON THE BUSINESS...

When asked to contribute a piece about professional wrestling I realized that there was so much that one could expound upon that it would almost be impossible to pin down one topic.

Who's your favourite wrestler?

What was your favourite angle?

When was your favourite era?

A fan could go on and on listing their likes and dislikes about the business. But I thought that seeing as I once worked behind the scenes and had an insider's knowledge at how things worked it would be an easier list for me to write. I was wrong. Once you sneak a peek behind the curtain it is hard to become objective about the business, so I won't pretend to be.

Here is my list on what I think the business needs now. These are my thoughts and my thoughts only. They do not reflect the opinions of anyone else. You can agree, disagree or disregard, but these are what I feel are a few of the issues that should be addressed.

The Future

Every sharp businessman not only has his feet planted in the "now" but his eyes looking toward the future.

A smart wrestling promoter should do just that. Everyone knows that the business has changed over the years and with the demise of the territories and smaller promotions fading into obscurity it is of the utmost importance that the next generation of wrestlers are carefully cultivated and shaped to be able to carry on the tradition of the business as well as being able to take the business to new places it has not been before.

That means that if you see potential in someone in a smaller promotion that looks like he or she can work, wait to take him or her up into the big leagues.

Create Angles That Are Fresh
(Easier Said Than Done.)

And ironically most of the best angles have been rehashed (or rebooted if one is inclined to use that insipid word) from previous story lines throughout the history of wrestling. French writer Georges Polti once wrote a book that summarized that all storytelling could be boiled down to the Thirty-Six Dramatic Situations.

In wrestling we can hone those thirty-six down to just one. Good guy vs. bad guy (or in wrestling terms Babyface vs. Heel) that is what the business is all about. Now getting those two combatants into the ring is another story and storytelling is another intricate part of the equation that makes a good wrestling match/angle/concept.

Without going into the history of the business too much, pro wrestling and television were made for each other. It is a union that can be symbiotic at times and parasitic at others but wrestling and television is a collaboration that generations have grown up with and seeing that many of the first TV shows on television in the 50s were soap operas, that concept fell easily into the wrestling world.

Going to a wrestling match or seeing one on TV and seeing two wrestlers put on a great show is exciting, we marvel at the athleticism and showmanship that the wrestlers display in the ring. But once we get to know these competitors, once we see them in a story line or angle and we get to spend time with them it is impossible not to have an emotional vested interest in the outcome.

Now the match is not just a display of two highly skilled competitors putting on a great show of athleticism and showmanship; if done well it becomes an emotional release, a cathartic climax to an angle pushed to its limits. With that being said, what new angles are there to explore?

Polti believes there are thirty-six different ways to explore this, but I feel there are three essential ingredients that are indispensable to create an angle that can work.

Trust your gut. If you feel that something can work, then go with it. Don't listen to others who may have an agenda (and when dealing with other creative members in the Writers' Room - EVERYONE HAS AN AGENDA. And usually that agenda is not in your best interest) If you think a certain angle can be created, or reused or salvaged than try it out. If it doesn't pan out move on but it's better to try than not try. I have always said that wrestling fans have "short attention spans but have great memories" meaning that if you give them something they like they'll run with it even if it is something they have seen in the past. And if they don't like it they'll let you know.

Trust the wrestler(s). When you are dealing with wrestlers on a one to one daily basis you get to know what people are like, their strengths, weakness, abilities, goals and fears. By the time a wrestler gets to this level he or she should have some years of experience behind them. Use those years of experience.

Trust the fans. You will know real quickly if something you put together doesn't work. It's the fans you are catering to: never forget that. Without them there is no business. Don't try to alienate them.

Don't Dwell On The Past
- But Don't Forget It Either

There tends to be trend of looking back fondly on the business (which is something I do often) and remember the halcyon days of our youth when we first started watching wrestling. Nothing compares to those first matches we saw as a kid and captured our imagination. And no wrestlers loom as large in our memories than the first superstars we were first captivated by.

But sometimes we tend to reach back to the past to bring out some of our old heroes for one last hurrah. But one last hurrah leads to another hurrah and then another hurrah and yet another one and soon we have wrestlers on the equivalent of the continual never-ending KISS farewell concert tour.

Wrestling should always respect and remember its roots but those roots have spread out and from them, the business we have today has grown from their contributions.

Move Out Of The Spotlight And Gives Others A Chance To Shine

This is geared to a certain few people in positions of power in the business. If you had your time in the sun, made your money, made your mark then it's time to move on and let someone else have a chance of grabbing the brass ring.

But unfortunately that is not the case: some wrestlers cannot stand the fact that their time had come and gone and they will do anything to maintain their spot on the roster. For many of the performers in the business all they know is wrestling. Stepping away from a profession that had millions of people cheering (or jeering depending on the wrestler) is hard for anyone to accept.

It is a very special few that can go by name recognition in any profession, and even fewer those who have become legends and have the ability and financial security and just walk away from the adulation and more importantly the money. But it is like the old proverb of "flogging a dead horse": how much mileage do you expect to get out of certain wrestling personalities?

You can't blame the wrestler for all of this either.

It's up to the promoter to have the final say. It is up to the promoter and his creative team to come up with fresh new angles, and his road agents to cultivate new talent so that they are ready to step up and take the challenge when they are called upon. It has become a two-sided coin of frustration when trying to book a show or create an angle: you want to create something fresh and new that will excite the fans.

But what happens a lot of the time is that all the great ideas that are created in the writers' room fall flat when the talent is not there to fulfil what has been conceived. You just don't have the depth on the current roster: some of the newer wrestlers are still too green; the locker room has no experience.

These are some of the problems that bookers/promoters face and it's only natural that one would reach out to someone that has the experience, the talent. Some wrestlers stay around too long and in many ways it's because there is no one to take their spot, to fill the void that a legend leaves when walking away.

But the worst thing is when a wrestler of note ends up working in the office or behind the scenes, or finds themselves in a position of power either through buying a percentage of the company or marrying into the organization. This usually ends up bad for other wrestlers trying to work their way up. Backstage politics in any profession hampers and hurts business overall.

Cronyism and collusion do nothing to help advance business in a positive way. Backstage politics in pro wrestling is some of the worst I've ever seen and I've worked within the Hollywood system for years, so I've seen the apt art of backstabbing and treachery in action. When bad things happen behind the scenes in wrestling, it hurts what happens in front of the camera and in the ring.

But if you are always sticking around, always putting yourself into the mix, the product will never grow. It is bound to become stale and boring with the same old faces, the same old angles, the same old outcomes. Bottom line, if you can't breathe new life into the business, save your breath and step aside and let someone else have a shot.

Listen To The Fans, Embrace The Change Of Time

This goes to one of my early points: listen to the fans. If they are clamouring for a certain wrestler or angle odds are they are probably right in wanting what they want. Wrestling fans are the most astute and well-versed students of their sport: they know what they want, and they know what works.

Do you think that ten years ago a C.M. Punk or Bryan Daniel would have made the WWE roster?

Especially with certain people in the position of gatekeeper who decided it was their duty to allow only who they felt worthy enough to be in the spotlight (this goes back to cronyism concept). If C.M. Punk and Bryan Danielson (along with the other hard working wrestlers around the country) didn't push themselves every time out and become fan favourites would they have gone as far as they have?

And it wasn't just their talent, hard work and dedication. It was their connection with the fans. And that union of wrestler and fan base is something that becomes unbreakable when created over a long period of time.

There's Too Much Damn Wrestling On TV (Did I Just Write That?)

Yes, I did write that and let me explain my case.

I hate being that guy that says "In my day", but "in my day" wrestling was on one hour a week on Saturday mornings and if you missed it, you missed it. No DVRs, no VCRs, no repeats. And that made it all that more important to catch that Saturday morning show and that is the same reason it made it all the more special. Wrestling fans made every effort to catch the show, and there was enough wrestling packed in that hour to keep you satisfied for the week.

Today the WWE alone has over five hours of wrestling on every week. That's a lot to ask, a lot to ask of the wrestlers, a lot to ask of the announcers, the road agents, and a lot to ask of the fans. And how much quality wrestling is weaved within that large smothering cloak of wrestling, enough to warrant five hours of airtime? When wrestling is done right, it's done concisely, it's done quickly and it has the fans wanting to comeback for me.

Today the Lucha Underground on the El Rey Network is an hour-long program and in that hour they pack a lot of great wrestling and interesting and innovative story lines in it. Championship Wrestling From Hollywood, same thing.

One hour a week, but within those sixty minutes this locally run show out of Los Angeles matches entertainment value minute for minute with some of the bigger promotions. Why are these one hour shows working out so well? They don't overdo it; they don't oversaturate, over permeate or overindulge.

If you were to slow down your DVRs when watching RAW (and I believe that is the standard for watching wrestling these days) how much time would you fast forward through? Probably a lot I imagine. And that's not good; it's wasteful. And when you waste time in television you waste money: not a good business plan.

Make every moment count.

Television time is a very expensive medium: every second needs to be accounted for so you should think about cutting back on the overexposure and putting the emphasis on the in-ring work, and then creating interesting angles and diverse, unique characters.

Now I know that no big promotion with a television contract is going to be cutting back on its own airtime. Too much is invested with contracts and commitments and sponsors. But it would be wiser to build a stronger product around a tighter TV schedule. You never want the fans to sigh "ho-hum"... you want them to scream "HOLY SHIT!!!"

RISQUE

SEX, LOVERS, INCEST, AND SEXUAL ORIENTATION...

BROCK LESNAR WAS PITCHED AS A HOMOSEXUAL

As incredible as it might be to picture this now, one of the initial pitches for Brock Lesnar was for him to play the role of a "badass gay" character. One writer wanted the OVW standout to be the WWF's first openly homosexual character, long before the likes of Chuck & Billy or Rico Constantino came along. The idea was to seek positive PR from the gay community by presenting Lesnar as a regular guy who happened to be homosexual. It was a marked contrast to how the company usually dealt with this sort of sensitive gimmick. Just look at their portrayal of Goldust as a predatory homosexual who stalked members of the roster and sexually assaulted them. Not to say they wouldn't have done the same thing with Lesnar, but fortunately/unfortunately we never got the chance to find out. The idea was rejected out of hand by Vince McMahon and practically everyone else involved in the creative process, and instead given to Chuck Palumbo and Billy Gunn later in the year.

RIC FLAIR - DIRTY GRANDPA

At the tail-end of 2000, Stacy Keibler revealed to the world that she was pregnant, launching one of WCW's most notoriously awful angles. She swiftly followed up her happy news with the bombshell that on-screen boyfriend David Flair WAS NOT the father!

In the absence of a fitting adjudicator - like Jerry Springer or Maury Povich - that led to an awful First Blood DNA match at Halloween Havoc pitting David Flair against Buff Bagwell, who he thought to be the father. If he won the match he got Bagwell's blood and could prove he was the father. Or something like that.

Eventually, the whole sorry affair just went away because the crack writers realised there was no possible payoff. Instead they had Stacy admit that she had made it all up for attention. All terrible, but it could have been even worse.

Originally it was pitched that Ric Flair would be the dirty dog responsible for going behind his son's back and impregnating his girlfriend. That would have led to another sorry Flair vs. Flair family feud that nobody on the planet wanted to see.

Thankfully it never came to fruition, and equally fortunately, neither did Vince Russo's self-serving attempt to claim Keibler's child as his own in another alternative pitch. Like anyone on the planet would ever believe Vince Russo could score with a woman as hot as Stacy Keibler.

INCESTUOUS KEN SHAMROCK

For reasons best left unexplained, Vince McMahon and his creative team have had an unhealthy fascination over the years with one of life's greatest taboos: incest.

Back in the Attitude Era, Vince pitched the idea of Ken Shamrock having a sexual relationship with his on-screen sister Ryan. Shamrock rejected it out of hand saying he refused to do anything that would affect his children.

"I think Vince was a little upset with me. You know, I had to weigh it out and I thought kids at five, seven and ten-years old don't understand that this is entertainment. They look at it and they think it's fun and these guys get to beat each other up and all these things are happening.

"I just thought that me doing something like that and my children really not understanding that, I thought it would hurt them so I went to talk to Vince and I told him no. I got beat for three months straight after that so it didn't work out so well but I just couldn't do it."

Curiously enough, the "Shamrocks" actually dated in real life, so who knows how Kenny explained that one to his children.

THE BLONDE BITCH PROJECT

WWE can be incredibly vindictive when they want to be, especially when someone has the audacity to challenge them in public. When *Playboy* cover girl and star of the Attitude Era Sable quit the company and sued them for sexual harassment in 1999, Vince McMahon and his team of lawyers were not happy and immediately counter-sued.

Not content with just fighting the future Mrs. Brock Lesnar in the courtrooms, WWE also planned to use their television shows to poke fun at her. Vince Russo and Ed Ferrera shot a series of vignettes with Stevie Richards and The Blue Meanie entitled 'The Blonde Bitch Project', a spoof of the famous found-footage horror film *The Blair Witch Project*, which was popular at the time.

Essentially, Meanie would be looking for the "legend of Sable" in the woods, eventually stumbling upon Richards wearing a blonde wig and dressed from head to toe in Sable attire. Then it would end just as the movie did, with Meanie getting knocked to the ground and the picture fading to black.

Everyone involved was thrilled with the segments, but when they were shown to McMahon he didn't get it. He hadn't seen the movie—because he doesn't watch movies because he considers them to be a spurious use of time—and assumed that nobody else who watched *Raw* would understand them either. This, despite the fact the parody had already been mentioned in a *USA Today* article and that *The Blair Witch Project* was one of the highest-grossing films of the year.

THE BURCHILLS

While WWE may have pushed a lot of talented British wrestlers over the years such as Paige, Bad News Barrett and Davey Boy Smith, it is worth remembering that grapplers from the UK haven't always gotten a good deal in the company. Besides the evergreen William Regal and the aforementioned Smith, in truth few Brit have managed to truly establish themselves as genuine superstars.

Take Katie Lea and Paul Burchill, for example. WWE pursued the duo for years and, after all of the visa issues red tape was sorted, they were set to debut with big plans. Vince McMahon had plans for the underrated Burchill and his storyline sister. Very, very weird plans. He had long wanted to do an incest-based angle/gimmick (as evidenced by Stephanie McMahon's claims about him wanted to be credited onscreen for siring her baby) and now he was finally going to do it with the Burchills.

Paul and Katie Lea Burchill debuted on *Raw* in the spring of 2008 and it was going to be revealed that they were having an incestuous relationship. However, two weeks later, the company switched to their show carrying a PG rating and the gimmick was mercifully dropped.

MELINA THE MAN

In another WWE relationship angle that played on an existing relationship and put it through a grotesque filter, Melina accused Batista on *SmackDown* of "forcing himself" on her. Having seduced him in the locker room, she then turned on the big man during a press conference, threatening to take legal action. It was all very classy. And it could have been even more shocking. The angle was supposed to have a further stinging revelation, with Melina revealed to be a man in drag. It's safe to say the writing team were not fans of Ms. Perez. Stephanie McMahon turned the pitch down, worrying it would wreck Melina's career. After all, where could she go from there? Then again, it might not have been the worst idea. At the very least it would have made her more interesting.

SABLE 4 UNDERTAKER

In 1997, the WWF were formulating plans to make Sable a love interest of The Undertaker. In the lead up to the angle there was even an article in *WWF Magazine* drumming up some gossip by running paparazzi-style images of Sable and 'Taker conspiring at a cafe. However, the Undertaker's real-life wife did not approve of the storyline, so it was unceremoniously canned. According to Sable, there were also plans to have her manage 'Taker, as she appeared in *RAW Magazine* decked out in Undertaker clothing and his hat. But as soon as 'Taker said no, the angle was dropped without further discussion, such is the power he wields.

THE ORIGINAL WWE GAY WEDDING

When WWE arranged an onscreen wedding between Billy Gunn and Chuck Palumbo in 2002 they were roundly praised by the gay and lesbian community for promoting a positive homosexual storyline. That all changed when it was revealed to be a big hoax, with Billy and Chuck shooting in character and admitting that the whole thing was nothing more than a publicity stunt. Suddenly, those who had been praising WWE rapidly changed their tune. It was a classic bait and switch, but also one of the most memorable angles of the year.

But Chuck and Billy were not the first choices for a WWE gay wedding. Several years earlier the idea had cropped up, with tag team Too Much—Brian Christopher and Scott Taylor—the lucky pair selected for the role. The duo would go on to great success as Too Cool under the handles Grandmaster Sexay and Scotty 2 Hotty, but in 1998 they were still very much opening match fodder.

Vince Russo pitched the gay wedding storyline and things seemed to be heading in that direction based on the antics of the pair in their matches (who would often engage in linger hugs or smack each other playfully on the ass), but it never went any further. The story is that Jerry Lawler—Christopher's father—stepped in and asked for the angle to be dropped, but that is unverified and merely speculation.

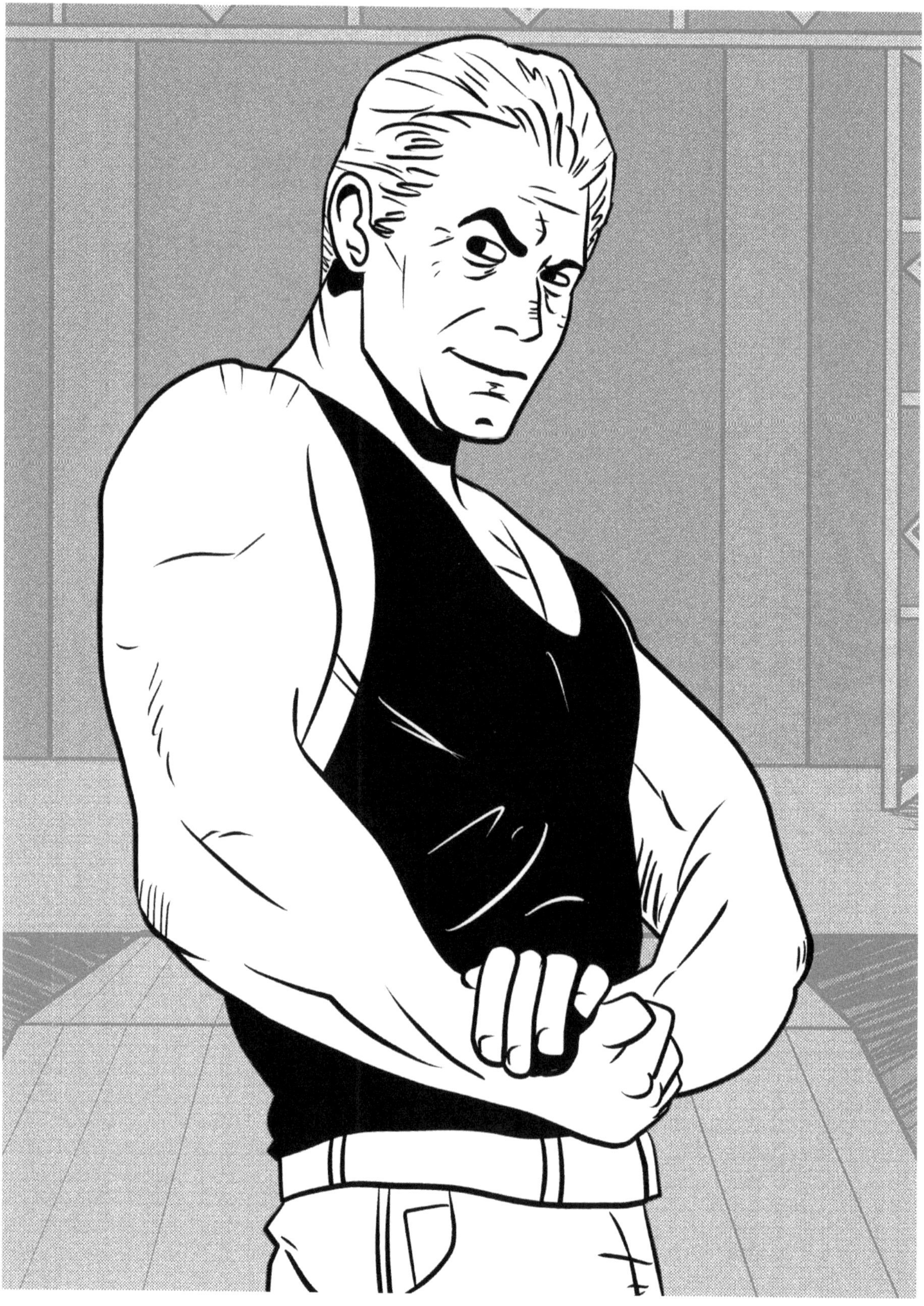

BATISTA - CHILD OF RAPE

On the list of 'issues to handle with sensitivity', rape must rank pretty highly. It's an awful, awful thing, and really if it's not dealt with in the correct manner it shouldn't be dealt with at all. WWE have been accused in the past of trivialising date rape with the Triple H/Stephanie wedding, but have managed to steer clear of the issue, by and large.

In 2002, however, WWE seemed to be on a crusade to offend as many people as possible. How else do you explain the fake Billy and Chuck gay wedding, Triple H simulating necrophilia with Katie Vick and promoting a segment called Hot Lesbian Action? Future Hollywood star Batista debuted on WWE TV in 2002 as Reverend D-Von's muscle, Deacon Batista. It was a poor gimmick, but it could have been a whole lot worse.

During his appearance on Chris Jericho's *Talk is Jericho* podcast, Batista revealed that his character nearly went in a very different direction. In order to explain why he was always angry, it was going to be revealed that Batista was a 'rape child' and that he was always angry because his mother was raped and he never knew who the father was.

Thankfully this never made it into Batista's backstory. It could have been a career-killer.

OWEN 4 DEBRA

Yet more WWE marital unrest almost came in 1998 when the creative team pitched the idea of Owen Hart having a secret affair with his tag partner Jeff Jarrett's valet Debra. The revelation of the sordid association would tear the tag-team apart (stop us if you've heard this one before). Hart had other ideas though, and rejected the storyline because he didn't want his wife and children to see him in such a negative light. Rumour has that his reward for this act of defiance was being saddled with the comedy Blue Blazer gimmick, which ultimately cost him his life. A hefty price to pay for sticking to one's principles.

VINCE 4 STEPHANIE

There's a worrying trend of proposed incest storylines in WWE that were canned before they made it to the screen. Even more worryingly, they came straight from the top. One such example saw Vince McMahon propose a scandalous sexual relationship with his own daughter. When Steph was pregnant, Vince pitched the baby being the product of his loins. Steph was repulsed, commenting, "I don't know who would find entertainment in a storyline like that." When Steph said no he then pushed for Shane to be revealed as the father instead, because there's nothing like using your family and making a mockery of their real relationships to sell PPVs. Steph said no way, and the issue was dropped.

GOLDUST'S BREASTS

"Know what Goldust wanted to do one time? He wanted breast implants." - Vince McMahon, *Raw* March 26, 2001. Ultimately, Vince McMahon used Goldust's desire for breast implants as an opportunity to joke, but the story was actually entirely true. Runnels formulated the idea to make the character even more of a freak. In truth, Goldust was on the endangered list at the time and he needed something that would save his career. Vince Russo confirmed the story, claiming that Goldust would have gone through with it—and allowed WWE cameras into the operation—for $1 million. Vince apparently genuinely considered it before changing his mind at the last minute. Ultimately it goes down in history as one last desperate gasp of a character scrabbling for survival.

FEATURE:

BY GEORGE J. RUTHERFORD

THE WISDOM OF DUSTY RHODES

While working as a creative writer, one of the most rewarding aspects of the job was harvesting the stories and collective knowledge of the road agents, writers, "mechanics" and other old-school talent.

For me, a five-minute discussion with Howard Finkel or Sgt. Slaughter rivalled the excitement of watching a main event match in front of 14,000 screaming fans.

Undoubtedly, the most memorable of these experiences was an educational one-on-one chat I shared with the late, legendary, American Dream…Dusty Rhodes. It was 2007 and Dusty was the head writer of the ECW brand at the time.

In a rare quiet moment, Dusty and I were in the writer's room on the fourth floor of Titan Tower. We were talking storylines, match booking and finishes. Dusty must have felt like imparting some knowledge to me because in the midst of our discussion he said (and I shall do my best to write it the way he said it):

"Let me tell ya somethin' young fella. The day that professional wresslin' reached the point of no turnin' back was the day that Vincent MacMahon (sic) went on national television and told the world that what we do isn't real."

Essentially, Dusty explained that the entire way the business was handled, from publicity to creative writing to match choreography had to be changed once people knew everything was scripted. A wrestler couldn't build tension by working a sleeper hold for two minutes because people now know the guys in the ring are just catching a breather. The stunts had to be bigger, the moves riskier and the show much more spectacular if audience attention was going to be held.

As silly as his character often was, the man himself had a phenomenal understanding of the industry and transformed my entire outlook on wrestling in one short afternoon.

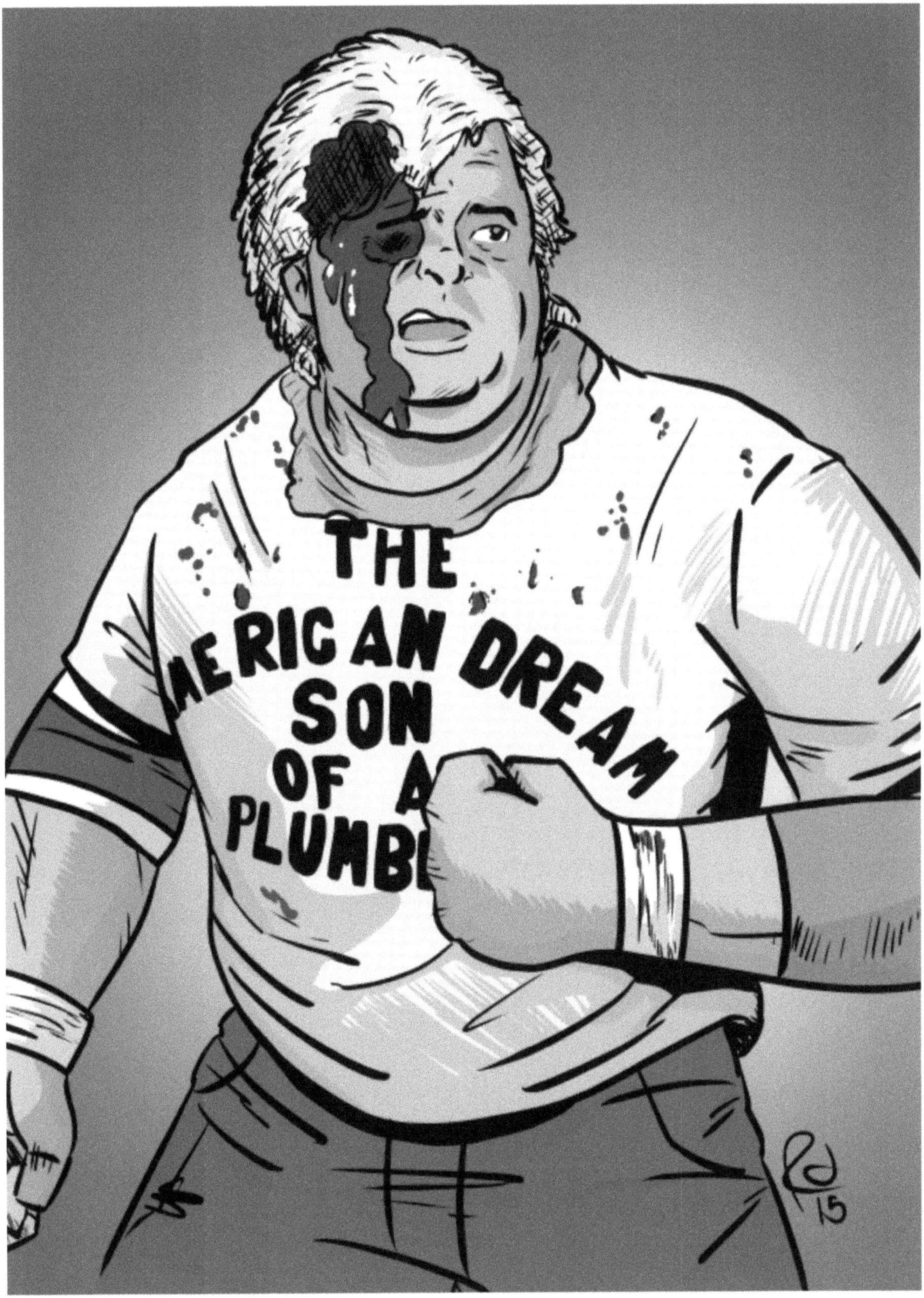
THE
MERICAN DREAM
SON
OF A
PLUMB

DEFECTORS

THE TALENT MOVES THAT ALMOST HAPPENED...

THE BRITISH BULLDOG

Two days after he headlined the WWF's infamous Beware Of Dog pay-per-view opposite Shawn Michaels, Davey Boy Smith faxed Vince McMahon his ninety-day notice. His intention was not to leave the WWF but rather to force McMahon's hand into giving him the main event level contract he felt he deserved. However, once Eric Bischoff got wind of his availability he was eager to make a deal.

By the time Bischoff came to the negotiation table he had debuted the nWo angle on television to a phenomenal response, with the success driven by the unpredictable nature of recent former WWF stars turning up and pledging their allegiance to the renegade faction. Smith would fit the bill perfectly as the group's latest addition, and WCW were so confident that he had been wooed by their deep pockets that they earmarked his debut for the September 2nd edition of Nitro.

But Smith did not want to return to WCW. He had suffered a torrid time there in 1993 and had actually been fired by Bischoff over a monetary dispute, so he had little interesting in working for him again. Davey Boy's loyalty was to the WWF and upon surveying the wrestling landscape he realised he was in a better position in New York than he would be in Atlanta, despite personal assurances from Hulk Hogan that he would be looked after.

Eventually Smith turned down the WCW offer and re-signed with the WWF for $250,000 per annum guaranteed. Little over a year later due to the fallout of the Montreal Screwjob, he was forced to pay $150,000 out of his own pocket to tear up the contract and quit the WWF to follow Bret Hart to WCW.

SHAWN MICHAELS

In July 1997, Vince McMahon met with Shawn Michaels to discuss his return to work following a Hartford locker room bust up with Bret Hart in June. The miserable wrestler begged McMahon to let him leave for WCW so that he could be back with his friends Kevin Nash, Scott Hall and Sean Waltman. He wanted to enjoy wrestling again, away from a locker room that despised him and specifically away from Bret Hart.

"Please Vince, just let me go," Shawn pleaded, "I am miserable. I am making everyone else miserable." McMahon was starting to realise that one of Shawn or Bret would ultimately have to leave the WWF, because they were so diametrically opposed that there would never be locker room harmony with both of them around. With Hart 40-years-old and vocally opposed to the WWF's edgy new direction, Michaels at 32 and one of those at the forefront of the WWF "Attitude" movement was the logical choice to keep around as far as he was concerned.

In addition to the ever-present tension between Michaels and Hart causing problem after problem, McMahon reasoned that if he didn't let Bret go then it wouldn't be long before the rest of his top stars, the likes of Austin, Undertaker and Michaels, would all expect contract parity with him. That would ruin him. Michaels had already complained about Hart's contract to McMahon, grumbling that he couldn't comprehend how a performer he felt he was better than was earning double the money that he was. Choosing Shawn at half the price would also remove the issue of Austin and Undertaker complaining about the disparity in pay, killing two birds with one stone.

Partly in an attempt to placate Shawn, but also because it was dawning on him that he needed to restructure Hart's deal or let him go, McMahon confided to Michaels that he had only signed the deal in the first place because he felt he had to. Everyone had told him it would kill the WWF to lose Bret, but the figures were telling him otherwise and he no longer felt Hart was worth the investment. "I don't think Bret is going to last his contract," McMahon admitted. "Don't worry, Shawn, we will make wrestling fun again for you," he assured him. Shawn agreed to return to work, and history would show he was one of very few grapplers never to cross the North/South divide.

THE ULTIMATE WARRIOR

Following the Montreal Screwjob and the loss of Bret Hart and Davey Boy Smith to WCW, Vince McMahon worried that he was lacking in star power on his roster and made a secret offer to The Ultimate Warrior in December 1997. Their relationship was strained following their split in 1996, but Vince was desperate and felt the return of Warrior could boost *WrestleMania XIV* like it had *WrestleMania XII* the last time he returned two years earlier. McMahon offered Warrior a five-year contract guaranteed for $750,000 downside per year, half that of the contract with Bret Hart he had fought tooth and nail to get out of. In his letter to Warrior offering the term, McMahon wrote the following: "Jim (Hellwig), this deal is far more lucrative to you than our last agreement of 1996, and obviously, far more long term. I look forward to building the resurgence of the Ultimate Warrior again. Vince." Warrior ignored the offer from McMahon and instead signed for WCW a few months later for an even larger sum of money. As predicted by everyone in the industry, he caused headaches, flopped, and quit his contract early.

GENICHIRO TENRYU

Long-time WWF fans will remember Japanese wrestling legend Genichiro Tenryu teaming with Koji Kitao against Demolition at *WrestleMania VII*. He also competed in the 1993 *Royal Rumble* match, and the next day, Vince McMahon held a press conference where he announced that Tenryu would be competing at *WrestleMania IX* (against Jerry Lawler), and that the WWF would be sending talent to WAR in Japan (which Tenryu ran) later in the year as part of a cross-promotion between the two companies. Somewhere between then and *WrestleMania* the decision to have Tenryu wrestle at the show was nixed, and the WWF didn't work with WAR until May 1994. Tenryu did return to the WWF one final time though, competing in the 1994 *Royal Rumble* match.

MACHO MAN AND HULK HOGAN

Often wrongly claimed to have occurred in 1997, Hulk Hogan and Randy Savage were both in talks with the WWF towards the end of 1996. Having recently turned heel for the first time since the birth of Hulkamania, Hogan was red hot following a difficult few years in WCW and McMahon once again saw the value in having him as part of the WWF.

The pair met in Denver and discussed terms, with Hogan later claiming that McMahon offered him $5 million per year to return in the Royal Rumble match – a bout he would win – before going on to lift the WWF Championship for a record-extending sixth time at WrestleMania 13. As with every Hogan claim, the fee and the scenario are fanciful at best, but the rumours that they were negotiating and Hogan was close to signing a deal to return were true.

Randy Savage intended to come with him. He and Hogan were involved in WCW's main event feud at the time working opposite one another, and Vince wanted to neuter WCW by snapping up both members of their top program at once. However, Hogan did not fully trust Vince and suspected he would be punished for testifying against him in the steroid trial, so he backed out of the deal, robbing fans of the chance to see him in dream matches opposite the likes of Bret Hart and 'Stone Cold' Steve Austin. He had been using Vince for leverage more than anything, cleverly increasing his perceived worth to Bischoff by openly discussing McMahon's interest with his current boss.

With the Hogan deal off, Vince's interest in Savage waned. He had not seen the value in Savage as a main event star in 1993, never mind three years later, so he refused to offer him anything other than a short term wrestling deal which transitioned Randy into an office position. Savage was not interested in that and the deal broke down, with Savage too committing to WCW for another three years. It was the final time he and the WWF negotiated and he never wrestled or appeared for them again.

NFL STARS

Professional wrestling has a rich association with professional sports, with some of the finest grapplers to ever set foot in the squared circle having tried their hand at other sporting pursuits first. Future wrestling World Champions such as Goldberg, Ron Simmons and The Rock tried their hand at football first. Others came from more diverse backgrounds such as Randy Savage (baseball), Ken Patera and Mark Henry (Olympic powerlifting), and Tom Prichard and Bad News Brown (judo). However, the ability to toss a pigskin, throw a ball, or punch the living daylights out of someone far from guarantees success in pro wrestling.

Following the WWF boom in the 1980s, a number of ex-pro sportsmen attempted to forge a quick and easy path to success by trading the gridiron for the wrestling ring. Amongst them were a number of NFL stars, such as tragic defensive end Lyle Alzado, and Atlanta Falcons offensive guard Bill Fralic.

Fralic was a curious case. In 1985, he was drafted to the Minnesota Vikings, but he did not want to play for them because of his view that they were "cheap", so along with his agent Ralph Cindrich, he concocted an entirely fabricated story that he was considering quitting football for pro wrestling. Fralic turned to fellow Pittsburgh native Bruno Sammartino to verify the story for him, leading to the Vikings trading Fralic to the Atlanta Falcons in exchange for Chris Doleman. It turned out well for the Vikings, as Doleman ended up in the NFL Hall of Fame for his time at the team. One year later Fralic did actually end up in pro wrestling as one of the participants in the *WrestleMania II* "NFL vs. WWF" battle royal, then turned up again in 1993 as part of the WWF's Yokozuna bodyslam challenge aboard the USS Intrepid.

Another who toyed with the idea of stepping inside the squared circle was two-time Super Bowl champion John Matuszak. His link to wrestling was via Paul Orndorff, whom he was teammates with at the University of Tampa. Orndorff suggested Matuszak try his hand at pro wrestling, but he chose acting instead, becoming world-famous for his role of Sloth in cult classic *The Goonies*. Sloth vs. Hulk Hogan? It was very nearly a reality.

FEATURE:

BY SCOTT CARLSON

10 WRESTLERS WHO NEARLY DEFECTED DURING THE MONDAY NIGHT WAR

At the height of the Monday Night War, *Raw* and *Nitro* were highlighted by an almost-weekly parade of wrestlers defecting from one company and showing up on the competition's program soon after. Think about some of the biggest moments from both promotions during that era: Lex Luger showing up on the first *Nitro*, Scott Hall interrupting a *Nitro* match, Chris Jericho interrupting a Rock promo, and the Radicalz taking a seat in the front row at *Raw*.

Defections were the norm in the mid-to-late 90s through to the closing of WCW in early 2001. Look at the WWF and WCW rosters from those days and you'll find plenty of examples of superstars who performed for both companies (in Rick Rude's case, televised on the same night). But there also are several wrestlers who were either rumoured to or very nearly did jump ship at some point, only to change their minds and decide to stay put. All of their respective decisions had a huge impact on the Monday Night War.

Let's look at ten wrestlers who nearly jumped from one promotion to the other during the Monday Night War and see what their departures could have meant to the WCW vs. WWF battle for ratings supremacy.

Yokozuna (1997)

By the time the Monday Night Wars were in full swing, Yokozuna was on the downswing of his WWF career. But that doesn't mean that the former WWF Champion didn't have some value to the competitor. At that time, Vince McMahon and Eric Bischoff would have been gleeful at poaching any former World Champion, if only for bragging rights. With Yokozuna, the possibility of a rematch with Hulk Hogan (so Hulk could get his win back) loomed.

The possible defection was described by former WCW star Konnan, who was friends with Yoko. He spoke about how the former champ loved K-Dogg's character in the nWo and the idea was to have Yokozuna "come in as a Samoan gangster and have my back."

Scott Hall tried to facilitate a negotiation between Yoko and Bischoff, but somewhere in the process Yokozuna got offended at the VP's negotiating ability and the move never came to fruition. It's a shame Yokozuna never got that one last chance to prove himself. Instead, he last appeared on 1999's horrific *Heroes of Wrestling* PPV before passing away a year later.

Shane Douglas And Konnan (2000)

Okay, it might seem like cheating a little, but since 'The Franchise' and Konnan's near-departures stemmed from the same incident, it's worth lumping them together. In early 2000, WCW lost a significant part of its talent pool when Chris Benoit, Eddie Guerrero, Dean Malenko and Perry Saturn jumped together to the WWF. The foursome fled WCW after Kevin Sullivan—who they despised—was put in charge of booking, which was the last straw for them. They would debut in the WWF as the Radicalz and go on to varying degrees of success, with Benoit and Guerrero famously closing *WrestleMania XX* holding both World Championships.

But the four who left WCW weren't the only ones who tried to leave. Alongside the quartet were Shane Douglas and Konnan, showing solidarity with their peers and determined to walk out with them. However, for those two it was merely a bargaining chip to secure a better deal with WCW, as Douglas had heat with the WWF stemming back to his troubled 1995 run with the company, and Konnan had issues going back even further related to his planned portrayal of the Max Moon character in 1993.

There was every chance that Douglas and Konnan would have gotten WWF contracts, allowing Vince to really rub it in with half-a-dozen WCW stars showing up on *Raw* together. At worst, he could have brought them on for a few months during the Radicalz's initial run. After all, if there's one thing Vince loves more than holding a grudge it's making money. And the sheer numbers of six WCW wrestlers jumping at once could have been tempting enough.

Of course, that was about the last gasp in the Monday Night Wars, as WCW would be out of business 14-months later, and Douglas and Konnan would fade out of the limelight a little more.

The British Bulldog (1996)

Yes, Davey Boy Smith did defect from WWF to WCW after the Montreal Screwjob—and then jumped back to WWF nearly two years later—but the British Bulldog very nearly had one of the most significant defections of them all in 1996, almost jumping to WCW to become the fourth member of the New World Order.

In the WWF, Bulldog was battling Shawn Michaels unsuccessfully for the WWF Championship during 1996, so he was peaking as a main-event-level star just as the nWo was beginning its ascent. For Bischoff to secure yet another former WWF star so quickly after signing Hall and Nash would have been a major coup for him, and would have added much fuel to the fire about the nWo being an invading force sent from the WWF.

Instead, Smith showed his loyalty to McMahon and the WWF by signing a long-term contract with them. Bulldog would win tag team gold with Owen Hart and become the inaugural European Champion over the course of the next year, and he was part of the reformed Hart Foundation that dominated the WWF in 1997. So while it wasn't a bad decision to stay on, had he jumped to WCW Davey Boy would have been an early member of one of the most influential groups in wrestling history, which likely would have changed the course of his career.

Owen Hart (1997)

This one is a painful wishful thinking exercise for many wrestling fans, and Hart family members alike…

In the aftermath of the Montreal Screwjob, Davey Boy Smith and Jim 'The Anvil' Neidhart jumped to WCW with Bret Hart, ending the Hart Foundation. Bret's younger brother, Owen, would try to join the rest of the clan despite questions about whether WCW would even know how to use Owen on their stacked cards. Owen wanted to leave because of what McMahon and Shawn Michaels had done to his brother, but McMahon refused to let him out of his contract. He would remain with the company until his tragic death in May 1999.

Even if Owen had been able to leave, there wouldn't have been a full Hart Foundation reunion. As per the terms of their releases from the WWF, they were not allowed to form any incarnations of the Hart Foundation faction less the WWF would sue WCW for ripping them off, just as they had upon seeing Nash and Hall on WCW television playing practically identical roles to their WWF personas of Diesel and Razor Ramon.

Randy Savage (1996)

At *Halloween Havoc '96*, Macho Man Randy Savage lost a WCW Title match against Hollywood Hogan and then faded into the shadows, as his contract expired. Savage sat at home for a couple months before returning to WCW in January 1997 and kick-starting the last great run of his career, highlighted by his joining the nWo and his rivalry with Diamond Dallas Page.

But it was during his holiday that stories broke about Macho Man defecting back to the WWF after a three-year absence from the company. Savage returning would have lent some established star power to *Raw*, which was rebuilding around established stars like Bret Hart and Undertaker, with Shawn Michaels and Steve Austin bubbling underneath. WCW, meanwhile, boasted some of the biggest stars from the 80s and 90s WWF, and was in the midst of its 84-week reign in the ratings.

Had Savage jumped, he would not have been a part of the nWo, which would have created a vacuum in the earlier days of the group. There would have been no memorable feud with DDP—which elevated Page to a main-eventer—either. However, it never happened (as you can read elsewhere in this book), and Savage never worked for the WWF every again.

Hulk Hogan (1996)

A few months after reinventing himself and turning heel, making him relevant again after a shoddy few years, Hulk Hogan's contract was coming up for renewal. Hogan's timing in executing his turn to the dark side had been typically masterful, because now not only was he invaluable to WCW again, but Vince McMahon recognised how big of a draw he still was and wanted him back.

Hogan met with McMahon and talked terms, which included him coming back at the 1996 *Survivor Series* in Madison Square Garden as an unannounced member of a team (a role later taken by Jimmy Snuka), returned as a participant in the 1997 *Royal Rumble* match, and wrestling in the main event of *WrestleMania 13* for the WWF Championship.

However, Hogan did not really want to go back to working for McMahon—who he did not fully trust following years of bitterness between them—and instead resigned with Bischoff for the same lucrative deal he was already working under. Something that would have been a near impossibility prior to his turn.

Shawn Michaels (1996/97)

When Scott Hall and Kevin Nash left the WWF in summer 1996 and kicked off the hottest angle in professional wrestling, they also helped kick off 84 consecutive weeks of WCW winning the Monday Night ratings war. It also was perhaps the lowest point in WWF history. If a top star was looking at things dispassionately and only with his wallet in mind, he certainly would be tempted to jump to WCW for guaranteed money rather than go down with the sinking ship of the WWF.

For 'the Heartbreak Kid', the temptation was more than just money and ratings. Scott Hall and Kevin Nash were Michaels' best friends in the WWF, good enough friends that he and Triple H broke kayfabe with them in the infamous MSG Curtain Call incident. Michaels, who was champ throughout summer 1996, has since admitted in several interviews that it was "very hard" to resist the temptation to jump to WCW. While he acknowledges that there was never a formal offer from WCW, he does note that, "My buddies always said the door was open there."

While he sums up leaving WWF as a "brief thought" that he "quickly discarded," Michaels could be seen throwing hand signs to his buddies during promos (and vice versa), so he clearly had his friends on his mind during this period. HBK leaving for WCW in 1996 would have been devastating to the WWF and very well could have tipped the scales even farther in WCW's favour, perhaps to the point of no return.

Without Michaels, there wouldn't have been a D-Generation X, which was a major driving force not just throughout the Attitude Era, but also in the rise of one of the most important people in the company today, Triple H. How would he have fared without DX? Would he have followed Shawn out of the door? It's an interesting "What if?" question to pose.

Bret Hart (1996)

Next to the Outsiders, Bret Hart was probably WCW's biggest signing from the WWF during the Monday Night Wars. Sure there were other big stars who jumped, but Hart was the leader of the biggest heel faction in the promotion and the WWF Champion who was screwed out of his title on his way out the door. But WCW almost had him a full year earlier.

Hart was on the cusp of signing a three-year, $8.4 million deal with WCW in late 1996, but instead he opted to sign a 20-year contract to stay with WWF. It was a deal that Vince McMahon did not want to honour. The mammoth salary would end up leading to Hart's departure a year later via the Montreal Screwjob, at which point the WWF turned the corner and began rising from the ashes.

But what if Hart had signed with WCW in 1996? There would have been no legendary star-making *WrestleMania 13* match with Steve Austin, that's for sure. In fact, seeing as Hart personally requested a bout with Austin for his return at *Survivor Series '96* at a time when Austin was spinning his wheels, chances are 'Stone Cold' never would have been given the opportunity to break out of the back. Without Hart Austin would not have had that career-defining that made him into a superstar.

Ric Flair (1998)

In 1998, Ric Flair was engaged in a heated battle of his own with WCW over missing a show to watch his son Reid compete in a wrestling tournament. He was kept off television for months and slapped with a lawsuit as WCW president Eric Bischoff decided to make it personal with Flair. This led to the 'Nature Boy' countersuing and trying to get his WCW contract nullified so he could return to the WWF.

Granted, the 1998 version of Ric Flair was nowhere near the man who made a splash in WWF in 1991 (and even that Flair was past his prime), but aside from Sting, no man during the Monday Night Wars signified WCW more than Naitch, and Vince McMahon would have loved to have had Flair show up on *Raw*. Remember that even in late 1998, the WWF had only recently ended WCW's ratings dominance, and the battle was still see-sawing week to week. Big-time defections like Big Show, Chris Jericho and the Radicalz were still months (or more than a year) away.

A Flair defection would have represented a major coup for the WWF, much like Bret Hart was for WCW in late 1997. The difference was that Flair was a known commodity in WWF rings, a former two-time WWF Champion and *Royal Rumble* winner. Losing one of the biggest stars in the company's history could very well have been the death knell for WCW, accelerating the end of the Monday Night Wars.

In the end, it took an additional four years before Flair made his return to a WWE ring, which really is a shame, because a Flair/Rock feud in '99 would have been gold. But that's a story for another day...

BACKSTAGE

WHAT NEARLY HAPPENED BEHIND THE SCENES...

BRET HART WAS NEARLY PART OF THE KLIQ

The infamous WWF backstage political force known as the Kliq started out as nothing more than a group of friends talking about wrestling. Made up of Shawn Michaels, Diesel, Razor Ramon, 1-2-3 Kid and Triple H, the Kliq was initially a vehicle for creativity, but quickly morphed into a darker force. As the quintet grew closer to Vince McMahon and their opinion held more sway, their political machinations began to have a detrimental effect on the careers of others.

Changes in the WWF product soon reflected just how much influence the Kliq had amassed with McMahon. Pushes of the group's enemies were abruptly halted (just ask Bam Bam Bigelow, or Shane Douglas, or Mabel, or Chris Candido, or Jean Pierre Lafitte...), while simultaneously the Kliq members were given title after title in addition to key spots on the cards.

The Undertaker and his backstage posse were so irked by the Kliq's manoeuvrings that they decided to become an "official" clique of their own. Dubbing themselves the Bone Street Krew, Undertaker and his friends (including Kama, Yokozuna, Fatu and the Godwinns) served as a means to police the Kliq's activities in the locker room. It was the wrestling dressing room equivalent of *Gangs of New York*.

Even Bret Hart, respected company kingpin for so many years and a multiple time WWF Champion, was not safe from the Kliq's politicking ways either. In late 1994 and into 1995 he found himself shunted down into the midcard for uninspired programs with the likes of Bob Backlund, Jean Pierre Lafitte and Isaac Yankem DDS, while the Kliq enjoyed the fruits of the top card positions.

However, it could have been very different. Hart himself could have been a member of the notorious group. In mid-1994 Hart was still on good terms with Michaels, Razor and Diesel, and following a show in Hamburg, Germany they were all enjoying a beer together. With the drinks flowing and guards lowered, the trio floated to Hart the idea of forming a union consisting of just the top guys in the company. Their aim was to monopolise the top spots on the card and with it the money.

According to Hart, they wanted him to be the leader of the backstage group and the man who would voice any concerns they had to Vince. Backstage cliques were common in wrestling and Hart had seen similar unions in the past and knew they could be effective, but he was less interested in the prospect of hanging around with the three noted substance abusers every night. Plus, Bret was already the top guy in the WWF at that point. He didn't think he needed back-up to retain his spot.

WCW'S MILLENNIUM SHOW PLANS

As 1999 drew to a close, WCW were running short on viable ideas to help keep the company relevant. The nWo angle had fizzled out due to overexposure, and there wasn't enough lustre left in the battered WCW brand to retain the interest of the millions of fans they had made during their peak years. There was still a large fan base, but a lot of casual enthusiasts had once again turned their attention to the WWF, spearheaded by the record breaking Attitude Era. The Atlanta-based organisation needed something big.

One of Eric Bischoff's grand plans was to host a dual show that was part WCW wrestling and part KISS concert. The event would be aired live on pay-per-view to usher in the new millennium, which would have been an almighty gamble by the wrestling promotion. The main premise was relatively simple – WCW would put on a standard three-hour show, then KISS would play for a few more hours, just in time to celebrate the dawn of the year 2000.

It's probably a good thing that the whole project was scrapped, because it likely would been a huge waste of money. An earlier KISS concert live on *Monday Nitro* had cost the company a small fortune but only pulled a dismal 2.2 quarter hour rating, which was trounced by WWF *Raw*. In addition, WCW towards the end of 1999 were struggling to fill arenas on their own as it was, no less on the biggest New Year's Eve ever. This could have been a cross-branded nightmare for all involved.

RANDY SAVAGE TRIED TO BUY WCW

Given how little it cost Vince McMahon to pick up the wounded animal that WCW had become by 2001, you could be forgiven for thinking he was the only person who wanted it, but that was not the case. 'Macho Man' Randy Savage believed that WCW still had enough value to continue as a brand in some capacity, so he threw his name into the hat at the last minute in an attempt to beat McMahon to the punch.

"I was going to cut a cheque for that. I figured the WCW film library alone was worth that much money. I had a production company that was going to help me do wrap arounds, introduce all the matches, and send them overseas," said Savage.

Had Savage been able to beat McMahon to the rights, when other rival bidder Fuscient Media Ventures pulled out, WCW could have continued as a separate brand and challenged the WWF for a long time, providing much-needed healthy competition for the Stamford group, and providing an alternative place for the wrestlers to earn their livings.

Sadly, his bid came too late, and fans were robbed of the chance to see Savage and McMahon's personal grievances fascinatingly play out in the forum of corporate rivalry.

WWE BRITISH OFFICE

In 2007 there were plans in place to set up a WWE British office, with the intention being that the company would sign a host of British talent to contracts and mix them in with their lesser-used current roster stars, making for an UK-only version of what NXT later became. WWE went so far as to enter discussions with Len Davies' London-based organisation Real Quality Wrestling, with names such as Sheamus, Stu Sanders (Wade Barrett), Drew Galloway (Drew McIntyre), Brittany Knight (Paige) and Johnny Moss all considered as future WWE prospects. However, RQW was struggling to draw crowds and owner Davies decided to shut up shop before any deal was finalised. Instead, WWE simply raided the best talent and handed them development deals, with British talent becoming more prevalent in WWE in the decade since than ever before.

JOHN CENA WAS NEARLY FIRED

Say what you like about John Cena and the dilution of WWE's appeal to anyone over the age of around seven in the wake of the rise of PG programming, but his importance to modern wrestling is difficult to downplay. Incredibly, he almost didn't make it past the first hurdle. In several interviews Cena has admitted that he was almost fired by two high level personalities in WWE before he'd been given the chance to blossom: "Back in 2003, 2002, when I was just wearing boots and tights and I was supposed to be the "Ruthless Aggression" young good guy, nobody in the company liked me. I know Vince McMahon won't admit this, but he wanted me fired, Triple H wanted me fired. Everybody hated me. They just wouldn't give me a forum to showcase my talents. I've always been able to connect with the audience if given the ability to speak." Cena was saved by a European tour coach trip that Stephanie McMahon happened to be riding on. Some of the other wrestlers were freestyle rapping and Cena schooled all of them, drawing a big pop from the boys and from Steph. She immediately went to bat for Cena and vouched for him as a glorified Vanilla Ice clone. Not the best gimmick in the world, but at least it was something. And it obviously worked. Soon Cena embarked on the meteoric rise that eventually made him the company's top babyface for over a decade.

DIVAS SMACKDOWN

In 1998, in the space of just one year, the WWF went from a money-losing operation to a company pulling in over $56 million in profit for a single annum. The second boom period for modern day wrestling was well and truly underway, and Vince McMahon was keen to capitalise on the company's newfound success by expanding their weekly television output. One of the most important components of the WWF's success in the Attitude Era—if you believe Vince Russo—was the Divas. Forget your revolutions, the women in the 90s were purely there to titillate the fantasies of undersexed teenage boys. That's why Russo, idiotically, pitched that new UPN show *SmackDown* should be a Diva-only show. Despite the WWF having only a handful of women on the staff. Vince Russo - Attitude Era architect ladies and gentleman.

EUGENE ALMOST HAD A MOVIE

In their typically sensitive manner (that is to say, not sensitive at all) WWE debuted a "special" character called Eugene in 2004, getting a bonus dig in at Eric Bischoff in the process by making Eugene his nephew. Everything about the character is best left forgotten. The gimmick was roundly criticised, the writing was manipulative and offensive, and Eugene's very existence flew in the face of WWE's "don't try this at home" mantra that was so important. Even though the character was roundly despised, Eugene remained "comedy" writer Brian Gewirtz's favourite creation. Unthinkably, he even took a sabbatical to write a *movie* based around him. As noted by former WWE creative writer Alex Greenfield: "Let me say that again: Brian wrote. A. Eugene. Movie. And Vince *paid* for it… then locked the script in a box never to be revealed." Before the movie—which was surely brimming with political correctness—saw the light of day, Eugene was canned after portrayer Nick Dinsmore failed a second drug test.

THROTTLING VINCE MCMAHON IS BAD FOR YOUR PUSH

Vince McMahon was once attacked by one of his talents. No, not Bret Hart, this incident happened five years before the 'Hitman' decked McMahon in Montreal's Molson Center. This attack came at the hands of Nailz. Onscreen Nailz was a former inmate at a prison where the Big Boss Man worked, who claimed to have been beaten up by Boss Man while he was in prison. Now he was released he was out for revenge. Somehow he was the heel in all of this. Nailz savagely beat the Boss Man on an episode of *Superstars*, and the feud culminated in a Nightstick on a Pole match at *Survivor Series '92*. Following that Nailz was about to begin programmes with The Undertaker and (supposedly) The Ultimate Warrior, but he had a financial dispute relating to his shoddy payoff from *SummerSlam '92*. It is worth noting that Nailz received around $8,000 for his bout against Virgil at the show, which went all of three minutes and featured little more than Nailz choking out Virgil for the duration. Nevertheless, Nailz was furious and confronted McMahon, screaming at him in his office for fifteen minutes straight. When the WWF honcho failed to see his point, Nailz lost it, knocking McMahon to the ground and violently choking him out as Pat Patterson screamed for help. Nailz was removed from the building and immediately fired, which led to lawsuits from both sides. In his lawsuit, crackpot Nailz claimed McMahon had tried to sexually assault him during their discussions, hence the throttling. Nailz later testified against McMahon in the steroid trial and was so vitriolic and hate-filled that he ironically played a large part in getting McMahon acquitted. Don't expect a Hall of Fame call or a one-off return any time soon.

LUDICROUS REALITY SHOW PITCHES

With WWE Network figures becoming increasingly important, and other online service models flourishing thanks to original programming, it was inevitable that Vince McMahon would welcome pitches for original programming once the project got off the ground. Unfortunately for him, his creative team are not always the most original in their ideas. Among the ideas suggested:

- A WWE equivalent of *Dog The Bounty Hunter* featuring real-life bounty hunter Steve Blackman, for a show titled *Blackman's Bountie*

- *Pros vs. Joes* pitting WWE stars against everyday folk from the street. What did the writers think this was, the carnival days of wrestling?

- WWE's version of *Nanny 911* turning stars from the roster into self-help gurus (who in the hell would take life advice from a wrestler?)

- *WWE Dirty Jobs* which would see Superstars and Divas forced to do "disgusting and challenging jobs" As if watching The Big Show clean a inner-city school or Paige work a night-shift at Burger King somehow passes as entertainment.

WCW RAW

Perhaps the biggest plan that almost happened but never did related to the WWF's purchase of its rival WCW in 2001. Originally the WWF had intended for WCW to continue as an entirely separate wrestling promotion, but remain part of the WWF corporate structure. In some respects, this plan was an early prototype of what would become the *Raw* and *SmackDown* brand extension. The original plan—which seems bonkers in hindsight—was for the WWF's flagship show *Raw* to become *WCW Raw*, leaving *SmackDown* as a WWF-only show. When the respective television networks learned of this plan they balked and told the WWF in no uncertain terms that since they had paid for WWF content they expected WWF content. When Buff Bagwell and Booker T were booed out of the building during a "WCW match" on *Raw*, Vince McMahon realised the idea was an unworkable one too. The plan was scrapped and the WCW/ECW invasion angle was created as an alternative way of introducing talent to a WWE audience.

ECW ONLINE

Back in 2000, Shane McMahon wanted to buy the financially struggling ECW promotion, seeing the group as a test run for when he would eventually take over running the WWF from his dad. Obviously that didn't happen and ECW was morphed into the WWF the following year when Heyman went bankrupt and was forced to close down. ECW seemed dead, until one-off (WWE produced) show *One Night Stand* in 2005. Such was the overwhelming positive support for the show that Shane McMahon felt it would be an entity worth bringing back to life. Always at the forefront of modern technology, Shane's idea was to relaunch ECW as a web-only underground show, mixing in ECW originals with some newer names whom the WWF wanted to build for the future. Basically what NXT became once the WWE Network came along. Unfortunately for both Shane and wrestling fans, TV networks got wind of an impending third brand and offered WWE good money for a TV deal. Suddenly Vince was interested and took on the project for himself, leaving Shane hanging as he systematically set about forever tarnishing the legacy of the influential cult promotion.

Milton Keynes UK
Ingram Content Group UK Ltd.
UKHW051424120424
440949UK00018B/434